THE PERSONAL DIARY OF NURSE DE TRAFFORD 1916–1920

Edited by Martin Kevill

The Book Guild Ltd
Sussex, England

First published in Great Britain in 2001 by
The Book Guild Ltd
25 High Street
Lewes, East Sussex
BN7 2LU

Typesetting in Times by
IML Typographers, Chester, Cheshire

Printed in Great Britain by
Bookcraft (Bath) Ltd, Avon

A catalogue record for this book is available from
The British Library.

ISBN 1 85776 522 2

CONTENTS

INTRODUCTION

Martin Kevill and Nurse de Trafford were friends who lived in the same village. Croston Hall was demolished and, after 'Traffie's' death, her diary was found in the contents that he purchased.

In commissioning this book to be published, Martin Kevill hopes to show the sacrifices made by our servicemen and women in the Great War.

The dedication and commitment of the medical and auxiliary staff who tendered to the wounded is an example to all.

Grateful thanks to
Harris Library, Lancashire County Council,
Central Division, Preston for hospital
history and photographs.

Martin Kevill acknowledges the enormous help given by
Brian Crawford without which this book would not have
been published

AUXILIARY: MILITARY HOSPITAL, MOOR PARK, PRESTON

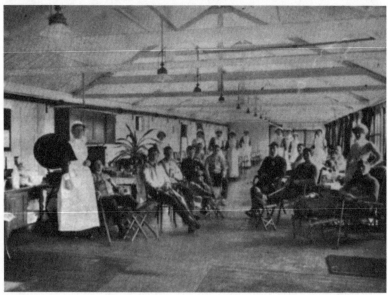

Moor Park Hospital

August 4th 1916

Time and time again I've made up my mind to write some sort of record – of hospital life – its works, its pleasures and its interests and its 'funny side o' things'! Our readiness to do all we can to help and cheer these lads (splendid fellows – that they are!) is our first aim and wish and we are rewarded amply for what we do – by their merry light-hearted ways and the gratefulness to their 'nurses' – which they certainly show at every turn. They are happy here – that I know and by the many letters I get from lads on my ward – and other wards into the bargain – I can tell that they've left us, not without upset – as one said to me before going.
'Nurse, I don't know how I shall survive tomorrow – leaving you all.'

* * * * *

I came here on Easter Sunday (April 23rd) – time though to feel thoroughly at home! I have been so far in 'A' Ward – all the time – the surgical one – and very much prefer surgical cases to medical ones – my 'Sister' (had the same one all the time) is a little ripper – and we get on well together – she's on her fortnight's holiday now (at the time of writing) – I shall be glad to have her back again – my 'Little Sister Boulton' – Sister Kirkham is now in her place – nice too – very, but give me 'Little Sister B!!' She wrote to me a few day ago.
'Friday 11th Sept. You go away for your fortnight – ? I must get you back again in "A" – can't do without you, lassie!' By the way, Sister B has been through the Serbian Retreat, went out to nurse typhus with the 'Scottish Women's Hospital' and has two medals.

Our hours on duty are 8 a.m. in the ward to 9 p.m. – two hours off some time in the day – and a half day once a week. The hospital now holds 184 men (with the tents) which have been put up a month or so ago and we are kept busy one way or another! For the first month or two we were sent men from Fazackerley Hospital – a dozen or so at a time – to fill up when we got short of them – since then we have had two large convoys from Rouen straight

3

from the Front – the first one 95 and the last 110. Great excitements, the '95 convoy' arrived at 5.00 and we were able to get them settled and comfortable by 8.30 or so. The '110 lot' didn't come till 9 p.m. and it was midnight when we left the wards (a long day 8 a.m. to 12 p.m., with a short two hours off). The '95 convoy' brought 14 stretcher cases into 'A' Ward to add to some we already had – which meant work!! They were an exceedingly nice lot of boys – a good sprinkling of Scotch Laddies – which I'd as soon have as any – dear bright cheery things and I could sit and talk and listen to their merry chatter for ever! 'Gordons', 'Argyle and Southerlands', 'Black Watch', 'Seaforths' – 'Scottish Borderers' – not forgetting the 'Highland Light Infantry' – we've had 'some of the best' from the 'HLI', good old 'Mack' (McKenzie) for one – was one of our nicest lads we ever had and my heart was very 'brok' (as the Tommies say) when he left us. Gemmell was another HLI – the 'Jock' of the Gordons – Bogey, bogey!! was a dear boy – everyone loved him but he was ours – 'A' Ward's.

'Does it hurt you Jock boy?' I used to say as I pushed packing with a probe into his ear, right through into the back of his head (diseased bone).

'No, nurse, it's all awa' now! It's a-richt the noo!'

All my boys I shall speak of – and put in some of their sayings – as I heard them – but I shall not want a written description to help me to remember them – I know every little inch of their characters and ways – each individually. We've had many 'send offs' lately and in two days 30 left – I suppose another convoy will shortly be arriving – it's as Gemmell said in his letter to me a few days ago:

'It's a case of patch and despatch these days – and receiving another lot before you're settled down properly – it won't give some folks time to get that sneaky feeling round their hearts and the want to settle down.'

This Highland laddie had been here months and certainly had the sneaky feeling round his heart, he writes lengthy letters to me.

'Your account as to how things were going on at Moor Park drew me nigh unto Preston,' he said, 'and I believe I did call "hut 21" a ward – there's no one to give me – or beg a pink carnation from here! We're having regimental sports tomorrow, so if it's your "half day off" – come along!!'

Now to another subject and we'll leave the 'HLI' alone for a bit. I have been in the theatre for an operation – 'Mac's' bone scraping – not a very long one – Drs Wilkins and Hadfield performed it. Dr H said while doing it – 'It's your first operation isn't it?' turning to me and then to Sister – 'most of your nurses have stood them well – not many have failed.' Of course I did nothing but watch – unbuttoned the Drs' coats – their long white ones – and helped to strap our 'Mac' onto the stretcher and went with them to the Ward and got him into bed – such noises and coughs poor old lad – he made before he came round. I was left in Galloway Ward with Fox (R's OL) when he had just come round from his operation, he was in agonies of pain and only half-conscious and shouted for water. I gave him his first sips of water out of a spoon.

'I'm going to get up!' he informed me and writhed about – like anything – I was glad to be relieved! Fox was better but Taylor (Shropshire LI) was lying unconscious – having had his operation four or five hours before he came round, 'Galloway' is a small ward holding six beds – but it's useful putting bad cases in – it is shut off from 'B' Ward and is quiet.

At the time of writing Whitehall (one of 'A' Ward men) is in there – been terribly ill – nearly died, had bad operation and on top of that – pneumonia – he was tapped and four pints of fluid were taken off his lung – they hope he'll pull through now – but he is exceedingly weak.

Talking of this ward reminds me of poor old Gutherie (HLI), he was dreadfully ill when he first came here – leg had been amputated and he had septic poisoning and pneumonia, he was an 'A' Ward man. We nurses, had to relieve his nurse (three of us in 'A' then, Foster, Arminson and self). Gutherie was constantly slipping down and every time one peeped into the ward, with 'How are you Gutherie, alright?' he would say – 'A'm slippin'!!' This meant four nurses had to be collected to hoist him up again – many a time we have had our caps nearly pulled off our heads – with Gutherie's huge arms as he levered himself up – each arm round a neck! How we've laughed at his quaint Scots sayings – 'Nurse, a'm dree the noo – give us a drink!', he was a man of few words – and hardly ever a please or thank you. 'Nurse, me peepe!' (pipe). 'The bool, a' want to spit.' Nothing but the bare facts did Gutherie give us!! He used to sit in a round air cushion 'Nurse, a'm no in the hool' and the job it was getting him in there – he was a big tall fellow, poor chap – rough and uncouth though he was – we did all we could for him. He used to eat most things in his fingers – our only patient that ever did – mercifully! Oh, to see him eat a poached egg in his fingers and all the yolk running down his chin and fingers! Also fish in white sauce was somewhat of a job – a dirty feeder – never a worse.

He got worse and worse – poor chap, only 27, but looked any age, older – thin, hollow cheeks and white as a sheet. I was in with him one morning – his breathing was terrible and he managed to say to me, 'Nurse, a've a cauld often, but never as bad a one as this' – half an hour after that he died.

His funeral, I shall always remember – such a hot sunny day – 30 of our wounded walked in procession (3 miles to cemetery), marched perfectly, though many of them done to a turn. The coffin was on a gun carriage drawn by six black RFA horses and a firing party was sent from the barracks. Twelve of us nurses met the procession at the cemetery gates – a space was left for us between our men and the carriage the 'Sisters' were in – and we fell in, in double file in step with the men. The staff and men, each gave a wreath.

A Preston VC died a short time ago – he was not at this hospital – but he came to see the men one day – his bottom jaw had been shot away – he was getting on well, but had a third operation and died under anaesthetic poor fellow. Our men collected £2. 6s amongst themselves – for a wreath – a huge red, white and blue anchor – a glorious one – they are so nice towards one another – and are as gentle and helping as any woman – to their fellow wounded. I've often watched them – I saw one bending over a man (just coming round after an operation) pleasantly the latter lifted his hand up to his pal's face and stroked it. 'A nice lad,' he murmured and looked up gratefully to him.

Another one's tea was scorching hot – his next door neighbour – leaning towards him said, 'It is so hot kid – let's blow!'

When new men arrive, our own lot will fetch and carry (those who are able) and say, 'Anything I can do for yer, chum?' They are BRICKS all of 'em and one gets very fond of the lads.

'Carry that for me – somebody!'

'Nurse, I would do anything for you!'

'You've lost that Rose – I'll hunt the hospital till I find it for you – nurse,' said one lad.

Our Ward 'A' is surgical and most of the men are out all the day – to see them (except those on crutches or in chains) one would say nothing was wrong with them – but wait till 'dressings' are done – holes clean through their bodies and deep wounds of every description. One lad (a 'Manchester') who's in 'A' now – Bedford by name – was shot through the shoulder – the bullet went on and came out just beneath his heart – the Doctor says it's an interesting case – by very deep probing he can feel a piece of splintered bone.

We've had with shrapnel and gun shot wounds – bursting bombs – trench buried men – frostbite – men that horses and gun carriages have run over and shot – RFA horses have fallen onto them and they are the cheeriest crowd you could meet in a day's march!

Still there's a bit of a cloud over this – in this way – an orderly told us that sometimes (I don't say often) a man will go away alone and sob, I suppose they feel broken and done for. It seems so sad that young lives should be ruined – man after man maimed and lamed for life. Such is War and I'm pleased and proud to be able to work amongst our soldier-boys all day long. Joyce is only 17 – he's a Dardanelle one – frost-bitten in both feet and they've been cut away till he has heels to walk on – nothing else – just little round stumps.

Lawton (S Lancs) left some weeks ago, he was about the same age – he could sport four gold stripes (for each time wounded) and wrote in my book 'Ready to go back again – with the best of luck', although two years under age. Topping little fellow – he was wounded at Viney Ridge while firing a Vickers gun on a mine occupied by Germans.

We have J Whittle (LN Lancs) in 'A' now – he's a champion heavy weight lifter and has won six World Records and ten for Great Britain (his heaviest weight 280 lbs) now he's got a shrapnel wound running right alongside his spine and when first done was 4 inches wide – he like many others will never be the same man again!

Stumps are beastly things to dress, we had a man in 'A' Frank (K's OYLI) who had hardly any leg left – it was amputated about a foot from his hip – it had dead bone in it too – and was sickening – it generally fell to my luck to bandage him up and he liked me to do it – said it kept up well when I did it – he was waiting for another operation and luckily got a transfer nearer his own home – we rejoiced when that stump went!

Coxon – has been in 'A' ever since I came (he's a 3rd Dragoon Guard) a very nice fellow – badly shot in leg – has had seven operations – he and Fisher (RFA) have been in hospital longer than anyone here – I shouldn't know 'A' without them.

I take Catholic men to church, sometimes, they are chiefly Irish Rifles, Dublin Fusiliers, Connaught Rangers and King's Own men – O'Toole used to come on crutches and hobble away and tire himself out – it's a mile to either church – St Ignatius' and the English Martyrs. The priests (English Martyrs) now send a conveyance of sorts to the men – drawn by two thin funeral horses – such a 'pleasure party' we look!

Nurse Anderton and I often walk – short-cut across the park to 6.45 Mass – leaving here 6.30 a.m. – we say in times to come we shall remember how we scuttled off (at 5.30 really – daylight saving on) over the best dewy grass.

We 'cubicle' nurses have quiet good fun in our 'den' – we have a second supper in there – cakes brought back from half days at home! etc. – Dolly Chase – when she was working here, used to keep port in the cupboard and china coffee cups which we drank it out of.

I'm called 'Traffy', 'Traffo' or 'Traff' by the girls and the Sisters too and get on swimmingly with everyone. I was away for a fortnight at the end of July and had quite a reception from the men when I returned – and heads and arms were shot out of 'A' Ward windows as I passed. A man from 'D' Ward – Turner (Lincolns) rushed at my small box and carried it down to my cube. I found that no new men had arrived in my absence – I was glad – as I passed through 'E' Ward the boys asked one if I'd come into it.

'Come into "E" this time,' they said coaxingly. I'm quite happy in 'A' and went back to little Sister B's room before she was dressed – and sat and talked on the bed with her.

'Of course you're in "A!" she said when I asked her, 'I don't care as long as you're back!'

When Jones (orderly) passed through 'A' later on – he exclaimed, 'It looks more like "A" Ward to see you back'!

We have concerts down in the recreation room and I play for them, also Nurse Powell and 'Nurse Kathleen' – and we've lots of good voices amongst the Tommies. Young Anderson (H Artillery Co) used to play the piano and violin too beautifully – he was in 'A' Ward, he used to play the violin in the ward just before the men went to bed – and they used to cluster round him and revel simply in it, so did the nurses – it was perfect – during these summer evenings and we did miss the boy when he went.

The boys often come back and see us after they leave – and it's nice seeing their bright faces – and hear them walking up the Ward with an outstretched hand – and a cheery 'Hullo nurse – how are you?' quite delighted to see us again.

'Nurse, I shall never forget what you have done for me,' said Sgt Springate (1/4 LN Lancs) before leaving. 'You are always at work,' he said to a nurse, 'and there's another down there on her knees (me) who doesn't mind work!'

Work! no – of course we don't mind it, they're worth it all. You must have a smile and a cheery word for each or you soon know about it!

'Nurse you never smiled this morning! You never spoke till 11 o'clock to me!' and poor you!, so unconscious of it all. They've always a merry little word or two ready as you pass up the wards – for instance picture me struggling along pushing a three-tiered trolley laden with dinner or tea things (I've had 24 or even more men to bring food up from the Kitchen – mugs, knives and spoons, plates etc.) a voice would suddenly call out from a bed. 'Heavy artillery coming up!! More ammunition!!' or trotting along with an enormous pudding (three times the size of an ordinary one) – some lad would say, 'Toss it up and catch it Nurse!' and a bit further another would sing out, 'Clap your hands, nurse!'

'When I get it there,' I would remark!

When the convoys came straight from France (like the three last ones have) – the men can't get over their food – how good it is to them, after bully and biscuits – they think it's heaven – one lad wrote in my autograph book:

'Appreciation'

'From "dugout" in France to Moor Park is a considerable way,
And when all the patients in this hospital today, are cured and
    well,
To fight – and God know, perhaps, soon forever there to dwell,
And some old wounds and illnesses come,
You bet – that if half a chance we got,
Again we'll come to you!'

No poetry in it, but there it is and it only shows Tommy's gratefulness – another boy wrote a similar 'poem' entitled, 'From Trench to Heaven', here's a sample of the verses in it:

'Up to your neck in water,
With little drops of rum,
But – when you get to Preston,
It's worth it! – By gum.
You're eating all the evening,
You're eating all the day,
They never give you "bully",
No – not they!'

and so on – anyhow as long as we know they're happy all is well.

The amount of food the boys 'put down' is astonishing – 20 quarts of milk a day – 40 loaves (and those mostly are long 2ft ones), the other day 70 rabbits were eaten for their dinner, beside about 25lbs of fish.

They are plain and outspoken these lads from the trenches!

'Nurse – I've got interjection!' (indigestion).

'Nurse,' one boy calls me to him one night. 'Can you give me anything to shift wind?' such a surprise, roared with laughter – and hurried off to try and procure the necessary dose.

The odd remarks I hear when taking the 'fish' and 'milk diet' round etc.

'More milk, nurse!' said Grundy (R West Kents). 'I shall mew soon!'

Planting a plate of chicken before Coxon (3rd Dragoon Guards) he said, 'I shall lay umpteen eggs after that.'

'I have no pain dear mother now,' he sang as he sat up to eat it – his dinner is helped down by tomatoes I bring him from Croston sometimes – he loves them.

'I don't care if it snows – now nurse, it beeeautiful, I'll tell you how battles are won and lost while I eat them!'

Grundy having tried on two pairs of grey trousers from the stores – I asked him if he now had one to fit.

'I've no stomach to keep them up,' he replied. 'You've taken it all away!' He'd been living on 'liquids' as he called it.

'They'll all be on liquids some morning,' said one boy – he meant changing the diet cards to 'Fluids', all down the ward. We are amused at a small boy who walked down 'A' Ward – he saw 'Fish' written on Coxon's bed and evidently thinking that was his name said brightly to him, 'Hullo Fish!'

The men are very funny when taking their medicines and pills – I gave some whisky-coloured stuff to Fox (K's O Lancs). Sgt Springate (1/4 LN Lancs) remarked:

> 'Looks like whisky,
> Tastes like whisky,
> It is whisky!'

Fox – 'Have some'?

Sgt S 'No, I don't want to be running all night kid.'

Fox goes on sipping it holding on to Reid's nose.

'Poor lad e's feverish, 'compris' that – never mind lad – we'll give you a funeral – a'll coom and help carry you out!'

'Parson talked of two climates after death,' said another lad, 'and e' sent two men's temperatures up to 102!'

Bray – (1st East Yorks) informed me – referring to the night staff – 'They come and push a clinical between your teeth at 3 a.m.'

Mills – 'I'd throw me hat at 'er if I was younger!'

Bray – 'I'd throw my boot at her!'

'Take me temperature with a hammer, nurse,' said Grundy, 'I'm dying – don't you ever wake up in the morning and find yourself dead!'

'Here's the thermometer – 97 and a bit, am I, put down the bit and leave out the 97 – I've busted it!'

'Nurse,' said Coxon, they wake me so early –you know that little night orderly, about as big as a three-penny bit – he came at 3.30 a.m., and I blow at 'im, and I never saw 'im again.'

One lad some nurse caught dipping his thermometer into his tea, to make it go up!

As I was saying before, pill-taking is a funny performance – I go round with the big brown bottle of cough mixture and a box of 'No. 9' pills.

'Anyone want a pill?' I ask, as I walk down the ward, hands will shoot up out of the bed clothes.

'I'll 'ave one Nurse!'

Some swallow them without water – some must have it, a Sgt Hoyle (Sherwood Foresters) can't get the pills down at once – he'll drink his glass of water and on my saying, 'Has it gone Sergeant?' he'll reply, 'The water has – not the pill!'

I asked a Scots laddie if he wanted water after his medicine.

'No water for the trooooops!' was his answer.

The boys always are in a lively mood – from supper time to roll call – to 9 p.m. when lights are put out – the wards are cosy and bright – well lit – and the broad striped red and white quilts look comfy and cheery, the walls and ceilings are all painted white and floor polished – when half (or more than half) of the men are out – in the daytime the wards look forlorn and deserted but now at this time in the evening the place rings with their bright laughter and they sit about in groups chatting and cracking their quaint little jokes one with another – it does one good to hear them.

One held up a limp cigarette, gone in the middle.

'Look at Nellie, what she brought me!' Roars of laughter. It doesn't take much to amuse them but it's all said on the spur of the moment and it loses it's funniest side being written down here – imagination must do the rest for those who have not lived for months in a hospital amongst wounded Tommies.

'Are you going to the fete tomorrow?' (fetie, as the Scotch lads call it) 'I'll pay for you nurse, on the 'obby 'orses.'

'Are you going in for the swimming competition Grundy?' I inquired.

'No nurse, the obstacle race and I think I'd be the biggest obstacle there!' Then Frank thought he'd chime in.

'I found the best shaped girl on the field yesterday, she's only 18.' Hair down?

'All the girls in Preston have their hair down up to 22!' These girls, these flappers!! What would Tommy do without them. Coxon would suddenly moan out: 'Me 'art's brok!!' to which Sgt Springate replied: 'Me 'art's been "brok" many times – get a bottle of sticotine and it's all mended up again!'

Coxon having returned from a motor trip with 16 other lads – I asked, 'Any Lillies at Lytham?'

'Yes nurse, flossies on the beach, with railway lines up their stockings an' it was raining, an' we wasn't allowed out!!'

Fisher (RFA) came down the ward singing. 'I'm in love,' he announced.

'Fisher's in love!' I told the others.

'Are you?' said Reid (A&S Highlanders). 'What's it feel like?'

'Spankin,' replied Fisher.

'Och awa' wi yer mon!' a Scottie would shout.

The gramophone would become husky and grate a bit. 'Mac'

McKenzie (HLI) going up between its doors put his head close to it and yelled, 'Is it a No. 9 you want, ah?'

Then Martin's 'Tom Foy' voice would begin: 'Rocked in the stable with the sheep . . .' They loved parodies to songs – they have many varied ones – there's one to the song 'If your heart may ache a while never mind . . .' Bren (LN Lancs) is constantly singing it, it runs: 'If the doctor says you're fit, Bren, never mind, and you've got to go to France – never mind. If there comes a blooming shell, that blows you into ——, There'll be nurses there as well, never mind!'

'Good night nurse' was all the go – especially when Gelder (W Riding) and Brew were together:

> 'Good night, nurse!
> Feel my pulse, it's getting stronger,
> Good night, nurse
> Hold my hand a little longer,
> Call me in the morning, if I get worse,
> Kiss your little patient,
> Good night, nurse!'

'Any more pills?' I still inquire through the chatter and snatches of song.

'Old pills, Lass?' says an HLI (Mac) – swallows one – 'Drat that lot!!!'

'Nurse, me bandage has slipped' from some boy – and to work on him! Coxon takes my photo I've given to 'Mac', and puts it under his coat.

'No,' I say, 'It's not yours,' and once more a pitiable voice unto the air.

'Me 'art's brok!'

As I make my way to Coxon to bandage his leg, he smiles – saying, 'Eh, I'm 'appy. I'm glad as you've come to do it – there are nurses and nurses!'

'Now me little nurse – I think you're safe to post these 'ere letters – there's "some intelligence" going in these!!'

Voice from Martins' bed – to Brew (both convalescent).
'Brew, I think you and me is going across the Channel again!'
Another voice joins in.
'Off you go, with the best of luck!'
'Back to the land,' sings another.

Someone must have sat on a prick – as I heard Coxon's voice slowly chanting ''E who sits on a tin tack – will surely rise!'

Mrs Smith (Commandant) comes rushing through the ward – on her way to the stores – in a little helter skelter rattling burst, the men watch her for a second or so and having got the time of her step – they start – humming and whistling –

> 'The Cambells are coming –
> Hurra – hurray!'
> and she finds herself a-marching!

I come up to a group of Scotties.

'Scots laddies nurrrrse!!' they greet me with – 'We shall think for you, when we've gone – it makes us want to do something for you in return! You're almost like a Scots lassie – rrrosy cheeks, darrrrk hair – we'll teach you Scots before we go.'

Rainey leans over to Stewart, saying as he looks at him, 'You're no so guid lookin' as you were – no so strrrrong!'

'A've got a sair head, (headache) nurse?' says another boy.

'Here's your medicine Reid,' I say – the Highlander swigs it off.

'It's wors than the last,' he says 'more poison among it! Give us a weeslucher o' water! – it's aricht the noo!'

A soldier goes up the Ward and turns into 'D' Ward to see a friend.

'Compris soldiers?' remarks Kent (RFA) from his bed.

The soldier's back looked humped.

'But 'e got 'it in front!' said Foster (North Fusilier).

Suddenly you'll hear an order shouted down the Ward (Stewart copies his old Coln') in a squeaky husky voice.

'Blackwatch! ---------- Charge ----------! Stand at ----------- ease!'

'Carry -------- Swords!' rings out a 3rd Dragoon Guardsman – whilst an RFA in a most determined voice yells, 'Men -- Cross your stirrups and ----- canter!'

Still another voice – 'Quick's the word – sharp's the motion – the order is – one! One, two!'

'This is a soldiers' ward, we're all soldiers here – compris that?' says some lad.

Cunningham sitting bolt upright, on top on his pillows exclaims, 'Anything doing in the sky line?'

When there is (i.e. when lovers appear at the end of the fence) there is tremendous excitement – their eyes nearly jump out of their heads – and they sit on the head rails of their beds straining to get a peep.

'Ah! – yer bad 'un!' shouted Sgt Philbin one night to a pair who'd been sitting in full view of the hospital for ages – it however made no difference, and the Tommies went on gazing with great glee.

Still snatches of song go on – from time to time – 'If the Sergeants pinch your beer – never mind!' a continuation on the parody already written a few sheets back.

'The Germans vowed they'd put the "Jocks" and Artillery into boiling oil if they caught 'em at Marnetz,' said Kent.

'And wouldn't we make a smell for 'em!' answered an RFA.

A man from 'F' Ward passes up 'A' – with a laugh like nothing on earth.

'Eh, nurse what's the matter with that chap – bet he must 'ave seen two whizz-bangs!' says a man. 'It's 'ere 'e wants it!' (pointing to his own head).

Two Tommies enter – with mousetraps (I said I'd give cigarettes to the one who caught the mouse that ate their toffee and things in their lockers). Rainey shouts at them.

'What the British Arrrmy coming to – catching rrrats in moose traps!'

The boys go on unceasingly – chaffing each other – at 9 p.m. – it often falls to my lot to put the light out.

'Fisher, where's your stick?' I say – groans from the men.

'Don'y turn 'em out, nurse!' but one by one they go out – as I pull down the incandescent lights chain with the help of the stick – and grope my way back to Fisher's bed with his stick.

'Goodnight to you all,' I say as I leave the ward – a chorus of

'Goodnight nurse' in every tone and pitch of voice – and I have done with 'A' Ward for that day! I pass through 'B' Ward on my way to supper and the lads I know there say a bright word or two and a goodnight as I go.

Hartley (RFA) had a toy mouse under a man's bed opposite to his – with a long piece of cotton tied to it – one night and as I passed he whipped it out letting it flash just in front of my feet – it had little wheels and a flexible tail.

'What's that?' I said, going for it and picking it up. 'What a ripping mouse – it's really good, where did you get it?'

'We wanted to frighten you, nurse and it didn't come off,' they replied.

'We did the same to a nurse just now and she really had a fit!'

Another 'B' Ward man said as I passed. 'I want to give you something!' and he put a little hot fainting frog into my hand.

'Poor little beggar,' I said and I dipped him into a fire bucket and let him go outside on the grass.

'And you didn't scream, you weren't afraid!' said Wooding (Northamptonshire Regt), quite disappointed.

Talking of supper – you sometimes find it ready cooked in the kitchen oven – and you go and dig at it yourself – shepherd's pie – or fish cakes – or as a treat, stewed rabbit in a big pot! Failing this, it means chewing a cold meat which has already found its way to the dining room – it's a funny procession trotting along each with our supper on a plate from the kitchen – sometimes we find a basket of eggs – left out for us which we cook, as we fancy ourselves – we're great hands at making buttered eggs and while one is stirring them – another makes the tea and eventually we enjoy a good supper and finish up (as I said before in this book) in the 'cube' sitting room – with cakes and chocolates etc. and a cigarette is not amiss!

One of the latest 'additions' to the hospital is a little revolving hut – summer house, to hold two beds – it has two windows and sides that let down – so that it does for 'open air cure' – it's nicely made and painted black and white to match the hospital – the sum of £20 (result of a children's concert) was paid for it. At present Bray (1st East Yorks) and Reid (A&S Highlanders) live in it – both boys belong to 'A' Ward, and it's 'A' nurses who have to go through the wet grass to get to it, with food etc. Their 'dugout' they call it – before taking possession of it these boys slept on the veranda.

The day the hut was finished I said, 'When are you going to take to your dugout?'

'I should like to begin now – but you canna take to the trrrrenches until it becomes dark,' Reid said.

They are very comfy in it however and are quite houseproud – and ask for flowers for it, when I come back with any. I tripped across there the other morning with Bray's cold milk, for lunch – he was asleep.

'Knock him up Reid,' I said and taking up a newspaper roll he proceeded to.

'Hey mon!' (whack) 'Hey mon! You must yell to get it sinkin' under 'is brrrrain – eh lad!' (as Bray began to move) ''ave a little cold milk!'

Bray opened one eye and saluted me.

Bray has a 'five tailed bandage', which I always put on for him (had appendicitis) and I trot out there when he's ready about 8.45 – to do it, when he blows his whistle! The bandage requires pinning in several places.

'Some bandage!' I remark as I wrap it round.

'And some nurse to do it up!' adds Bray.

Voice from another bed – as I pin it – 'Jar it into him nurrrse, I want to hearrrr him squeal.'

'We should be forgotten if it were no for you – out here,' says Reid.

I told one of the 'A' men to fetch some drinks for the hut pair.

'They've severrrred their connection and can get their own!' he laughingly replied!

Reid – by the way (now I'm talking of him) was the first man I'd seen tapped – for fluid on the lung – it's a brutal performance – such long needles to be thrusted straight at a go, right into the lung and the pumping and drawing the fluid off hurts dreadfully – the poor old boy went through a lot of pain – he'd had it done before so knew what to expect, he just doubled himself up and clenched his fists while Dr Wilkins made two separate deep stabs into him. I handed brandy to him to keep him going.

'I was afraid I'd shout,' he told us – but only a muffled groan escaped from him – plucky fellow.

* * * * *

This hospital is now under the 'War Office' and we get our new orders and that class of thing from the Barracks – we are directly under Fazackerley Military Hospital – Liverpool.

We have inspections – now and then – medical, and others – such preparations we go through to sweep up every particle of dust even in the darkest corners and places out of the way in case prying noses and eyes find any during their prowl round. General Sir Pitcowin Campell inspected us with a whole staff following – he was really topping to the men and they were delighted with him – I think he spoke to every man – he certainly did in 'A' Ward.

'Well, my boy,' he said to one of our lads, 'you've been shot in the arm?'

'Yes, Sir.'

'You better?'

'Yes, Sir.'

'Can you shake hands?' he said, holding out a gold-braided arm to him and in a moment Tommy and Maj. Gen. were shaking hands.

'That's right,' he said and passed to another bed.

'He's a toff,' said a lad to me. 'It's not often you shake hands with a Major General!'

The General made a cheery remark about a solitary boot that proudly took the place of a pair – its owner having no use for more than one – poor boy. These men (the 95 convoy from France) had only been in hospital about three days, they were told to stand to attention – all those who could. The General was delighted with the place and spent quite a long visit with us.

There is a Maj. Murray RAM from Fazackerley Hospital – he comes sometimes for the medical inspections and examines the men's wounds and dressings – escorted by the hospital surgeon and the Matron. These 'big wigs' are a nuisance – and give us a lot of extra work!

A Tommy said to me (after an inspecting officer had gone down the ward), 'Them sort is better outside!' and another lad watching the Gen. and staff pass the windows exclaimed, 'Generrrrals ought to be at the front – not enough there to manoeuvre the trrrrrroops!'

I'm glad to say what we called 'the early morning touch' is a thing of the past – for about six weeks – two cubicle nurses were called up at 5.30 – or about that time – to put in two hours' work, with the night staff – making beds, taking temperatures – washing and rubbing backs and that class of entertainment! Invariably you were told to go to help in a different ward to your own – I have been in 'D', 'B' and 'E' and only once in 'A'.

I liked 'D' at that time – they were a nice lot of men who'd been in hospital a long time and I always know a lot about the 'D' Ward men as they always pass through 'A' on their way. Some of the nicest were – 'Freddie' Close – Pearson, Gemmell, Fairbridge, Cavanagh – Schofield – Garner etc., – these boys used to like getting me for the early two hours! All went well – if the Night Sister, 'Sister Cullen', 'vinegar face' (even the sisters called her this) kept out of the way – she liked having a slap at us all in turn and easily got ruffled – she and Sister Brand (another night sister) are a pair and people to avoid!

I'll try and describe an early two hours in 'D' Ward – I pass through 'A' on my way to 'D' – my men greet me.

'Hullo Nurse – you're early – where are you going?'

'To "D".'

'Why that's not your ward!'

'I know it isn't, but I'm to be in there for the early two hours,' I reply and walk on.

I commence work on entering 'D' – chattering laughing crew as usual geet me.

'Good morning Nurse de Trafford! Did you get your feet wet?' inquire Fairbridge and Pearson.

'Did you come in a cab?'

'If Nurse de Trafford comes with us, on a motor trip we shall have fun!' says Cavanagh.

I get the temperatures finished with and charted – most of the boys are up – the breakfast has been brought up on a trolley by one of them and they are busy munching. Schofield still in bed, lazy bugger – I go to him.

'Get up Schofield it's late!' A mumble.

'Oh nurse – don't disturb the troops!' and he is under the sheets again.

'Pearson – I must do your back,' I say – he thinks a moment.

'Are those battalion orders – well – carry on!' he says.

Poor little Pearson, such legs he's got riddled with shrapnel – 30 pieces have been taken out – and 10 more are still in – he's only a young lad – 19 – he suffers a lot and sobs like anything under the bedclothes!

Shall I ever forget the morning Schofield upset all their tea on the floor the whole white enamel jug full (jug big enough for washing water). Tea! Yes, floods of it – swimming everywhere and he departed for the mop – in walks Sister Cullen!

'Why mop before you sweep?' she says in icy tones – all silent.

Schofield's voice 'Er – can you balance this jug on the trolley?' he says to her.

'Sister, the men have upset the tea,' I explain. I continue bed-making and washings and get finished in time for 8.00 breakfast, where I'm joined by the other 'cubicle' nurses who've been on a like job in some other ward. The other nurses come in.

'You two poor things – up early again this morning?' they say. 'Your week's nearly up – I wonder who'll be on duty at 6 a.m. next week?' and they anxiously watch for the new 'Staff list'!

One advantage is – you've finished duty at 6 p.m. – instead of 9 p.m. – when on 'early morning hours'. One 'early two hrs' I spent in 'E' Ward – one of 'D' men came to me.

'There is a Jock looking for you,' he said. (I knew who 'Jock' was – Gemmell!) He only wanted to ask why I was not in my own Ward. I like that! 'D' is no more my Ward than 'E' is. 'I'm "A"' I tell them.

'Gemmell is always up early when you are on duty,' says Teddy.

'Goodbye Gemmell,' I say. 'I'm off now!'

'When are you going – you're coming back in the morning? Going away for good?'

'Oh no!' I say.

'That's alright! You gave me a shock!' (hand on his heart) - that silly ass 'Gemmell of the HLI!' Talking 'E' Ward – I mustn't forget Pte Mudd – decidedly short in the baking – quite harmless, but a tile loose somewhere! – large head – small eyes and an odd-looking fellow altogether.

'I say nurse!' I heard a 'next door' Tommy call to Nurse Spencer. 'What do you put a chap like that next to my bed for?'

But they soon found out he was only simple – and quite good natured – 'Eh Mudd!' they used to call – to try and pull him up, and make him stop and talk. Mudd replied with a grin and a wave of his hand as he scurried on – but he'd plenty to say for himself. Before he started walking (he'd been gassed), he used to be brought to the recreation room – where some of us nurses would be playing the piano and singing with the men – they'd plant him on a bench and there he'd sit with his toes turned well in – till someone fetched him. How ever did they make a soldier of him! He used to sing and chatter away as he got better – I heard him singing something about 'milk pails' as I passed through 'E' Ward one day – and a voice from the opposite bed said, 'Better if you was in the milk pails!'

'Have Mudd in the "Black Watch" ,' I said to Stewart!

'No,' he said. 'We no want him, we're all soldiers in the Black Watch!'

Mudd was discovered one evening – no boots on – coat off – no cap – giving an exhibition of dancing before the railings to an admiring group of girls.

'E' Ward was a sort of zoo at one time – every man could imitate some animal and extraordinary good they were. How well Campbell crowed like a barn door rooster – O'Toole a barking colly dog – Thomson (a drummer lad) did cats and kittens and dogs, others imitated cows – and there was an excellent thrush – who warbled away beautifully! Funny crowd those 'E' men.

Thomson was a comedian – by profession – and was the life of the place – he'd a particularly good voice too – and danced well and was a ventriloquist into the bargain! So he was in much demand. He taught me how to summersault cigarettes off my nose into my mouth! To add to my accomplishments!!!

Dean (1st LN Lancs) was in 'E' – a very nice boy – also Faulk, Haydock-Bagot, Refford, Garwood etc. so many have been, and are still in 'E.' I can't mention all – it's a nice bright ward – about 30 beds – I like it next to 'A'.

'F' Ward is one I don't care about (the Medical Ward) it's so far off and one doesn't get to know the men – until they get out and about – if you notice a new man (you've never seen before) pass the windows – you at once say 'He must be an "F" man.'

Sister Gould ('Tiny') is in charge of 'F' – she's huge in height and breadth! Weighs 16 stone. It's amusing to watch the faces of the new men in 'A' Ward, as 'Tiny' passes through, for the first time since they've been in hospital.

'Eh, she's a big 'un. I never saw a bigger woman!' She's got a bright happy face though.

Durham – one of 'A' men (in Scottish Rifles) remarked, 'She's a big 'un, but a treat to go out with!' She's a good hearted soul – with the strength of a man!

A party went to the theatre and she picked up a lad without feet in her arms and carried him up the flight of stairs (Theatre Royal) to the dress circle! Sister Boulton went to the Whitsuntide Fete with her in Preston and she would stand and read the posters outside the 'Fat Lady's' tent – Sister B hurried her off – frightened to death she'd be taken for the Fat Lady.

*　　*　　*　　*　　*

I spent a day in 'E' Ward once (filling a nurse's place who was having a day off). I never heard the end of it for some time! My 'A' men kept coming through on their way to the recreation room.

'What are you doing here?' they demanded.

'I've asked Matron to transfer you back to 'A'.

'Look here – this won't do!'

But it had to 'do' for that day – and I was back in 'A' next morning.

Now just a word or so about work – it sounds all play by what I've already written. It's not all play and if it is hard work at times, all the men's brightness and little light-hearted sayings help one immensely – besides they are ready to give one a hand in many ways and it's always 'Alright nurse, I'll do it!' if one asks the least thing.

I leave my cube 8 a.m. or soon after – and as I go through the recreation room – well known voices call to me.

'Good morning, Nurse!' and a billiard cue is held high. Cassels and Faulk meet me with smiles.

Cassels – 'Good morning, nurse you're the only girl I ever loved!'

Faulk – 'Ditto here!'

I get clear of the billiard room – cup in one hand – empty hot water jug in the other, Dean (of the 1st Gloucesters) meets me at the top of 'E' Ward – and gets into step and escorts me as far as the door of the Ward, nice cheery beggar. Passing through the men's dining room I soon arrive at the kitchen – where I deposit jug and cup, and eventually get to the nurses' dining room where I eat a somewhat scurried breakfast – and read my letters (time permitting!). Into the wards at 8.30, we begin our day's work – I often start on scrubbing and sterilising about 15 bowls – this I do in the 'A' Ward washing room, 'wash house' (as the men call it) and a tight fit, the men are in there at this hour – not much room for me and my bowls! – still they get done somehow – there are about eight washing basins and three small looking-glasses – and there's great competition as to who shall get them for shaving operations!

I generally find a 'lamp-post' of a Grenadier, planted before one, face smothered in soap – the others too have been appropriated – some men are washing, some cleaning their teeth with tremendous vigour (a habit acquired I'm sure by many since coming into hospital) and spluttering all over the place!

Another man may be cutting a man's hair – in the middle of the room – busy hours these!

'What are you doing lad?' said Tommy one day to the 'would be' barber – 'Trying to remove 'is ears up 'igher?'

Stray songs reach me from the bathrooms – why do men always sing in their tubs! I'm thankful when 'bowl washing' is done, then back to ward work. There is the trolley to do and arrange – the senior nurse's job – that is, polish the glass top – and fill all bottles – sterilise all probes, forceps, syringes and instruments – Dr's and

Sister's gloves – fill up large bottles with swabs and medicated gauze (which have previously been sterilised). I take it in turns to do this 'trolley' work with Nurse Wilkins (we now have 'A' Ward jointly with one nurse under us).

There are the flowers to arrange – water to change – dead flowers to sort out. Medicines to give out, etc. then towards 9.30 lunches to fetch – but two of the men will as a rule get these – Sgt Hoyle (Lanc. Fusiliers) and L/Cpl Stirrup (Royal Fusiliers) and Knight (RRR) are very willing workers in this line.

The men keep changing so – in a few weeks' time their places will be taken by others – many and many a time I've got lunches for myself. Between 9.30 and 10 a.m. Sister Boulton comes on the scene, and dressing, commence. She does the morning ones – as a rule – and 'Wilkie' and I hand her instruments, and mix the eusol – and make carbolic or eusol fomentations as she wants them – I always do a lot of the bandaging – and get the old dressings and bandages down ready for Sister to begin – they often stick and require bathing off – poor laddies, they try and do anything rather than let you know you're hurting them.

'Sister,' said a '3rd DG' one morning – 'Me feet is long – like that – and wide – the rubber (on new leg support) 'as marked me leg like operation cuts – an' me toes is black!'

All this of course was exaggerated and half invented – but he was a depressed Coxon that day – a year with a leg of that kind would depress most people – he'd had seven operations and has long slits some of which are still open and running. Some days he's as chirpy as anything.

'Nurse,' he says to me. 'I've got a little friend today, a little 'ole – just 'ere – see? Running a little, a little bullet 'ole – an' it may not 'appen for months and months.' (All the while sitting up stroking his leg and examining the ''ole' that's started running!)

'There are legs and legs – and I've got a leg – me 'art is brok!'

I pass to 'Mac' (McKenzie HLI).

'I'm the only victim for Dr Hadfield today, Nurrrrse,' says he cheerily – 'Polish up the prrrrobe an' the sinus forceps!'

Yes, poor old 'Mac' he knows what a probe is like – I've seen Dr Hadfield push a probe deep into his bad hand and leave it sticking up in it, while he went and fetched something else – he may be a good Dr, but he is rough with the men and hurts more than he need.

If Mac saw a man doing something I didn't like – he'd say – in his 'rolling R' way, 'Stick a prrrrobe into him, nurrrrse, an' tour-rrrrn it rrrrround and rrround!' to pay him out I suppose!

Then comes Tweedy's turn to have his hand dressed (he'd put his hand up to shield his face from a bursting bomb and had got it bad poor chap. When he first came his hand was the size of three – and he'd a bit off his nose too!). Tweedy is a funny clown and keeps us in fits of laughing – he'll sit up there, in bed – after I've undone his nose bandage – with the eusol gauze dressing – just hanging, stuck by a corner, from his sore nose – grinning from ear to ear and his eyes twinkling – he shakes his head (the dressing swinging from his nose).

'Compris a nose?' he says trying to catch people's eyes.

Fisher (RFA) stands in front of him.

'Bomb couldn't 'a missed your nose, is as big as a box o' dominoes!' he politely remarks!

I then proceed to unswathe his bandaged hand – yards of it! – and a mass of cotton wool after that – I lose one of his fingers.

'Where's it gone?' I laughingly say, as I unearth it from the depths of the wool.

'I think 'e's listed,' he replies with a comical glance at me. I get the 'hand and arm bath', and leave my friend soaking in it for a long while – it's boiling hot at first and he holds his hand well out of it under the macintosh if he can – but I keep an eye on him!

'Compris – hot water?' I hear him muttering. 'See?' he says (when he takes it out – all white and washer women-y). 'See, you've boiled all freckles off an' all, anyone want any soup or stew?' he plays with his useless finger. 'See that, chaps,' he says 'You've fittled 'im, 'e's papoo! 'E's seen better days – compris that por lad!'

He's a funny fellow – Tweedy – he didn't get up for some time after he arrived from France and I used to tuck him up in bed saying, 'Go to sleep and rest a bit.'

'I think I will,' he'd say – 'Just for badness, just for spite!' and again his twinkly eyes would smile up at me, it would be a job to offend him!

I get to a Scotch laddie's bed – 'Oh – dearrr – another day in bed – ma wound is no healded yet' – 'a'm gettin' rrrrrestless in bed the noo – a'd like to be up an' awa' fra here!' This 1st Bat. Black Watch longs for his Perthshire.

> 'See that soldier Sergt Major
> Clinging to 'is 'orse's mane
> 'E will never make a rider
> If he tries & tries again'

sings an RFA.

'Not so much noise there,' says Sister B, 'and put your cigarettes out please while dressings are going on!'

Two 2nd Battl Welsh Fusiliers sit side by side to have their dressings done – Forest's second finger newly amputated and Gibson's little finger fracture and nearly hanging off when he first arrived! These two were in the same battalion, fought and were wounded together – came on same hospital ship and train and now have beds next to each other in 'A' Ward! They are great pals. 'The Big Gunner' has gone now (Surtees by name) – oh! those carbolic fomentations he required – I'm glad he's off our hands and well again.

Mills (Liverpool Scottish) has to have his wounded elbow squeezed out.

'Compris blood?' I hear our friend Tweedy saying (in his bed opposite), 'Compris being wounded?' The 'compris' comes into all their sayings just now and expresses a lot – I always think.

'Compris an open air shirt?' says Brown (Sherwood Foresters) as he pulls at the many tapes that tie up his slit down sleeve (holds his wounded arm). A large chunk has completely gone, blown away by shrapnel size of half an orange – exposing the sinews and nerves – a raw gaping deep hole.

These are samples of the smaller wounds – and the way the lads bear the dressings of them – the worse ones won't bear description – I've seen many a boy quivering from head to foot – uttering hardly a word – and scarlet in the face and perspiring freely – clutching the head rail of the bed with both hands – with an occasional 'Stick it lad' from the Dr.

I've seen four or five little operations done in the ward with a local anaesthetic – like removing shrapnel, opening up a wound, or putting in stitches. This makes work for us – as beyond the usual cleaning up of the trolley and sterilising dishes and ordinary instruments – we've got to boil up eight knives and needles etc. Besides, a Dr who means coming at 11.00 will invariably arrive just as we are clattering up with the men's dinners and then there's upset! Hot water rushed for, dressings undone – macintoshes spread out, out comes the trolley again and once more jingles up the ward.

When the ward is full of men in bed – the dinners are pushed up by two of us girls – large dishes full of stew and enormous puddings and are helped out in the little kitchen belonging to the ward, otherwise we bring up a few dinners on plates helped out in the kitchen. Dear! How they eat when a convoy arrives straight from France.

'I do nothing here, only eat and sleep!' one wrote in my book, and they really do improve visibly with good food and it's a pleasure seeing them enjoy it.

After the men have got their dinners – it's our turn – there's two 'staff dinners' the first at 12.30, the next, about 1.00 to 1.15, then back to the ward – those who are up are preparing to go out – the 'wash house' is once more a busy place – such scrubbings and hair brushing going on – they are tying each other's ties and titivating up generally!

'Nurse, can you make a good job of this?' A sergeant brings up his greatcoat to have his stripes stitched.

'Nurse, will you give me some khaki thread and a needle?'

'How does my tie look – will you put the safety pin in my collar for me?'

Up comes a 'King's Own' (Fox) 'Nurse – will yer pin me collar summat like this, don't prick me spine!'

A great deal of discussion as to the best cap badge goes on as they sit working and polishing their own particular one.

'Wait till you see my own buttons on my greatcoat,' remarks Martin (Scots Guards).

'Now this is the badge to wear – we're all soldiers in my regiment!' says another man.

28

They must cost something to the Government in polish I should say, judging by the amount they use – and blacking too – their boots must shine like nothing on earth! Eventually they sally forth, and are gone from the hospital till 5 p.m. tea time.

We nurses get two hours off, usually in afternoon and evening – I generally stay on – and keep an eye on 'D' Ward as well as 'A' – with a bit of work in between – such as ironing and washing and rolling bandages – taking empty bottles and charts down to the dispensary, showing 'visitors' round – arranging any flowers that may be brought and at 4.30 – ward teas must be fetched from the kitchen, this keeps us going – 4.45 is first staff tea – then back to the wards and work begins already described.

We've been in want of a hospital 'mascot', Quick (orderly) got a big brindle bull dog, the other day – the owner was drunk and took 15/- for it – 'Jack' is quite at home here now ('John Bull' to give him his right name!). Before my time, they had a tame goat – it used to follow 'Quick' about even into the hospital – the goat is no more alas! – on Xmas Eve he found a bowl of dirty dressings – ate them – and died – small wonder! No more animals except cats – and they let us know they're there at nights! Cat-a-walling – a din of a noise they make! I hear the Canadian geese too, to advantage. My 'cube' window looks out onto a portion of a very long lake – which is really in the park – just over the hospital enclosure railings – about eleven of these geese fly and go wheeling round and round over the roof in the early hours of the morning. I rather like to see them, one feels one's in the country. There was a 'small duck shoot' one morning – I woke up 7 a.m. – with the firing of guns. I pounced to the window and watched two keepery looking men try-ing to make white call ducks fly – they potted one close to my win-dow – I got quite wound up with excitement – I didn't expect to be present at a 'shoot' in Moor Park – attired in a night gown too!

We have artillery shooting by the way of a change – fairly shakes the place! '18 pounders' – they fire just behind a belt of trees in front of the hospital and break the mantles on the gas! Lately the firing has been stopped owing to some of the men having 'shell shock' – poor fellows they shook from head to foot – when the

29

guns started. They have driving practice every day – the batteries look well – good teams too – I enjoy watching them passing, I like being there when they are bringing the guns into action – such are the doings of these wartime days! About 10 or 11 a.m. they like doing firing practice.

'Keep your heads down lads!' you hear (boom).

'Look out boys keep below the parapet!' (boom).

'That's the stuff to give 'em!' one Tommy says to the other as they snoozle into the pillows in peace and comfort. They tell me they often dream they are in action and wake up feeling for their rifle, with the cry of 'there – they're coming!' and they sweat and get into such a frenzy – only to sink back and and find it is just a nightmare – and they are safe and well out of reach now of the Bosches!

*   *   *   *   *

Now let me try and describe the arrival of a big convoy (one that has come straight from France) – there is something strange and thrilling about it – to think that the lads have really taken part in one of these 'big pushes' one reads about and that in a week we have them with us – so fresh from the Great War – with all its horrors and miseries.

The last two convoys came from Rouen – they'd been for a day or so at the Casualty Clearing Station – had their wounds looked at and dressed and been inoculated against tetanus. Most of these men were fighting in the big offensive July 1st round Mametz. We received word they were coming – about 9 a.m. And that we might expect them that evening. Then to work! And work with a will – I remember well how Martin (1st Scots Gds) and I made bed after bed, and an extra job they were – as macintoshes and draw sheets had to go on most of them. Even the gramophone sung out lustily 'We're going to have a big night, tonight!', and so it proved to be. The 'A' Ward men set to with a will and helped us no end. Wood (Northumberland Fus) helped me to carry out about 20 vases of flowers.

'Oh what a game this shiftin' is,' he said.

'Each carry two sandbags and we'll soon get done!' a man with one leg said from his bed, as he watched me sweeping the ward.

'If I'd two legs on, nurse, I'd sweep the dust up as often as you'd like!'

A certain number of the men were turned out into the new tents to make room for the fresh lot of wounded. They took pillow slips and sheets off their beds – which meant rigging up the beds with clean ones – and the empty lockers had to be lined with clean paper – we had to sterilize a whole lot of gauze swabs and surgical dressing materials – new charts to be dated and put up – all this, and more – besides our usual work. About six sergeants and a Sgt Major were told off to see the ambulances arrived in proper order. Before 9 p.m. we got the beds prepared – turned back – from the sides to receive the stretcher cases – another nurse and I snatched a bit of supper about 8.55 and got back in the nick of time to hear 'Here they are!'

Then the procession began – 14 stretcher cases came into us in 'A' – khaki, French mud and sand – kilts bespotted with dirt – they kept arriving! Some pulling up, others being carried through to 'D' Ward – through all their weariness and fatigue – there was always a grateful smile (as we set to work pulling off their filthy clothes – washing them and getting them into clean things and fresh cool sheets) a smile of content – as they realised it was indeed 'Blighty!' Once comfortable a cigarette was the next thing – their dirty kits are rolled up – tied into bundles, labelled and carried off to the stores – these are disinfected and put away till they leave hospital.

The same night they arrive, we give them cards to address to their nearest relative – saying that they have got here 'Moor Park Hospital' – some can't write, poor lads – and we do it for them (owing to their wounded arms and hands). They are usually dead tired and fall asleep. Some of the surgeons come round and question them about their wounds – but the first dressings are generally done next morning, as most of them have been done on the hospital ship – those 'first dressings' they are a sad sight – gauze soaked through with blood is peeled off the wound. One after the other – they stick badly and require soaking – limbs are swollen and bad coloured – and are most offensive sometimes – at least the diseased bones and running wounds are and it requires all one can do to 'stick it' – not the 'sight' but the smell!

31

To go back to the 'arrival' – it is a weird procession of vehicles! Tradesmen's conveyances, vans, laundry carts, every conceivable thing – but we have not sufficient ambulances to bring the wounded up from the station – so the above mentioned are very handy – even if they only hold one stretcher case!

'What did you come up in?' I asked one wounded lad.

'The bread cart, nurse, I had it all to myself!'

Sister sent me down to the reception room to bring up the 'A' Ward patients – at least I escorted the stretcher bearers and showed them the bed each man was to have according to what doctor the patient was to belong to. The reception room would be a sight for an outsider to see – men sitting all round on chairs – tired, weather-beaten fellows – in soiled, muddy uniforms – labels tied to their button holes as to the nature of their wounds – written out by the Dr at the clearing station. Many lads without caps or kit bags – no time to look or think of those when the RAMCs were picking them out of shell holes and dugouts – in all probabilities under fire. I find the lads have a great respect for the RAMC and can't speak too highly of their devoted work of rescue under the terrific shell and rifle fire.

The stretcher cases are laid out on tables and the Matron – Senior Sister ('Sister Woodfin') and the hospital surgeon go round examining labels to see which wards to send them to.

'Dr Fraser, "B" Ward,' one hears and a tired pale laddie passes you with his stretcher bearers.

'Dr Murdock, "D" Ward!' here may come a limping boy – helped by 2 orderlies – supporting him as he tried hard to walk and show that it 'doesn't hurt.'

'Dr Healey, "E" Ward!' says the next – a bright eyed finely built boy started to move forward and follow the 'E' Ward nurse – his head is swathed in bandages – he walks with a firm, smart step – and a limp sleeve is pinned up to his coat. Another boy's 'done his bit!'

The next, 'Dr Sellars, "A" Ward!' This sounds like my man and I beckon to the stretcher bearers, 'This way!' We pass through 'B' Ward on our way – what a rough mess the ward's in – piles of khaki lying all over the floor, nurses running and scurrying, others pulling at a 'newcomer's' socks that refuse to leave their owner's feet, old patients helping to wash new ones – getting sore arms out of coat sleeves – undoing knots in boot laces – unwinding yards of puttees there seems unending work for everyone and you doubt very much whether things will ever straighten up again.

My man and I have arrived. 'Dr Sellers' I say to an 'A' nurse and we go to his side of the ward. The bronze Scottie manages to roll himself off the stretcher with our help – on to his bed – and I let his hand fall back gently onto the pillows – he is indeed a 'Fragment of France' – as we take his clothes and belongings away and undress him, he says with a twinkle, 'Me bits o' keepsakes – nurse – can I ha' them? They're in ma pockets' and diving in you find three or four cap badges – amongst baccy – some creased post-cards, a piece or two of shell or bullet case and other oddments beloved to Tommy.

He is slipped off the brown blanket we've undressed him on and slid into clean sheets – I take the chart down and ask him his name, regiment, religion – which I fill up. Having got the boys to bed and all their temperatures taken – we leave them to the 'night staff' and get to bed ourselves not before we are ready for it either! and return to find a ward full of fresh faces (cleaner faces too!) in the morning.

As I write this – I am expecting to hear the rumble of a fresh arrival of men – they were expected at 9 p.m. This evening but a later message informed us they wouldn't arrive till nearly twelve! So Matron packed us off to bed – saying we were to leave the 'housing' of them to the night staff and that we should have a very busy day tomorrow with them – 35 are coming – 70 arrived last week. So we shall be full again and we still have 80 or so old patients.

The old ones are really quite jealous of the new Tommies! Langley (Scots Greys) came up to me in 'A' the other day – he really belongs to 'D' but is banished to the tents being more or less convalescent.

'Nurse – do you still love me?' he said.

"Do I still love you Langley?' I replied laughing.

'Yes,' he said, 'in spite of all the fresh men?' pointing to the double line of beds 'but perhaps you've no time for that now!' as he looked back at me from the door, with that gay bright look of his.

No, we have a far greater 'love' (as Langley calls it) for our old boys – that we have pulled through aches, pains and sufferings!

Many of the lads have given me their photos.

'Here nurse,' said one, 'here's me photo, it would 'a been alright if me face had not slipped!'

They are very funny with their little sayings – Coxon asked me for my scissors the other morning – Whittle was sitting on his bed.

'I'm going to cut Whittle's nails,' he said and holding up a hand with decidedly black long nails he said, 'Are you thinking of starting spud plantin', cleanliness is next to Godliness – you've not got that, so try and get cleanliness!'

I find it makes a lot of difference how one asks the Tommies when you want them to help in the wards – I've never had any bother with them yet – one of them came to me the other day – Martins (S. Guards), he'd been told by a nurse who wasn't a great favourite unluckily! to sweep.

'She asked me to sweep up cigarette ashes I hadn't made,' he said – 'so I took a towel and went "biff biff" at it.'

I often have two Tommies to help me to fetch up suppers, we have to cross a passage when leaving 'B' Ward, before reaching 'A' and a voice rang out from a bed.

'Mind you don't get sniped nurse!'

Some of the boys have had bad toothache lately – it evidently reminded Schofield of his bad time with a tooth.

'Nurse, I had a tooth pulled out on the Peninsula' (he'd been to Dardanelles) 'and was pulled round the beach, whether it's the size of an elephant – or a flea – it's to come out!'

Foster informed us that he was a Salvationist the other evening.

'This is how it is' (he sat listening to Coxon) 'You throw a ha'penny on top of the big drum and say you are $11\frac{1}{2}$d short – where does the money go to! – The big drum don't 'alf 'elp his self! I'd like to see you with a big drum and a little red 'at!'

News of the big naval battle came in a short time ago – the Gramo'
was switched on to 'We've got a Navy! A fighting Navy!'

'Yes, Nurse,' they said, 'It's a good thing we've got a Navy –
there won't be much Army left soon!' Poor Army! It comes home
so much more at night – and I've heard other nurses say the same –
the lights are turned low and you gaze on rows of beds all full
of 'broken soldiers' – ward after ward – all lying there suffering
quietly and complaining so little. We have some truly awful cases
in now, much worse ones than we used to get, and we are often
tired out – it takes three or four nurses to do one dressing – 'I've
had many a pain, and nobody's seen it' – I heard a lad say, one day
– and it's the same all through – 'bear a lot and say little.'

'How are you Tweedie?' I said today (he'd had shrapnel
removed).

'Oh, I'm alright – a bit sore, me head is still on – "Compris" me
head still being on?'

We've started wearing stiff collars (October 1st) miserable things!
Whittle chuckled, saying, 'We'll see you in a dicker tomorrow!' (I
can't see now why a stiff collar would prevent me 'spitting out' if I
wanted to! He's an amusing love.)

Whittle (LN Lanc) a brother of the Whittle who was here nine
months – 'Always smiling,' he said to me today and 'How's our
nurse getting on?'

'You've three nurses,' I said to Kent (RFA).

'No,' he said, 'only one.'

'Yes – only one!' chimed in Bedford.

It's nice to feel the lads are fond of one and they constantly
show it – Gunn said this evening 'I'm always glad when they turn
you on to do me – you're good to me!' He has an awful dressing –
fractured arm with a great raw tear – 8 inches long by 4 wide, and
all the muscles standing bare like a lump of raw meat – with a big
tube about 5 inches long which has to be pushed up into it – I
generally support him, or hold his arm – while it's being dressed.
One night I wasn't there. 'I did miss you nurse,' he said, 'You give
me confidence!'

Fisher – the oldest patient here (bar Coxon) left last week – his goodbyes were many. Coxon will soon have been here a year – he says we shall have to fly the flag half mast when he goes and he won't go yet – he's to have his eighth operation on Sunday – poor lad – Sister Boulton, for chaff said – 'We're not friends, Nurse Myers shall do your dressing tomorrow, I shan't!'

Coxon turning appealing eyes to me said, 'No Sister! – Nurse de Trafford can do it, Nurse de T. and I have never fallen out yet!'

It's quite funny without Fisher, he and Coxon were great pals – he got into his khaki and dragged in kit bags singing, 'Pack up your trouble in your old kit bags and smile! smile! smile!' This is more of a military hospital than ever now! – the men even get their 'discharge' or their furlough (ten days before rejoining their regiments) from here now – instead of going to Fazackerly Military Hospital – which we are under.

I had an awful time with Tait, today – he is desperately bad – shot internally and we fancy the sciatic nerve is damaged – I was alone on duty in the Ward and had to get Sister Kirkham to help – (Sister B at pictures). He had spasms of terrible pain and groaned and moaned – and at last sobbed – his legs are all curled, can't straighten them, poor little fellow – he's a Northumberland Fusilier. We've another man Burke – same regiment – both leg bones badly fractured and a wound as large as a tennis ball on his shin – 3 or 4 inches of dead bone has been removed – I saw the Dr do it. Burke says his sergeant and Tait were the first men to fall in his company.

We have two Canadians in 'A' and a man in the Australians comes to have his head dressed – a large cut through his scalp – near shave – he's a nice fellow – so 'spick and span' with a big tuft of ostrich plumes – at the side of his colonial hat. Our new lot of Tommies who've been in ten days are getting up a bit now – very wobbly on their feet and they walk arm in arm, up and down the ward – the case of 'The blind leading the blind!' Gunn said, 'I don't think I shall be able to waltz so much by Christmas,' to which Marshall answered, 'I don't care whether I can waltz or no, as long as I'm in Blighty!'

36

Marshall is a 'Royal Scot' – from Dundee, such wounds – his thigh is torn open in two places and each is the size of a saucer (no exaggeration) – raw meat is the best description I can give – with the skin hanging down and you can syringe right through to the other wound – this passage is packed with gauze every night and morning – it's a 'nasty one', but these things make no difference to me.

We've a boy in the 'Suffolks' – Hood (by name) – he's got a big gaping wound on his shoulder – all the bone behind his ear has been cut away and you could push, and hide, a golf ball in the hole – it's so deep you could see the carotid artery beating away – it's making up from the bottom and sides now and doing well – his eye has been taken out – this, he says, was split right across – they operated on him in France – we had him here about a week after he was wounded.

There is a man in 'D' Ward now – he suffers frightfully – and keeps asking the other lads there, to bring him razors etc. – so that he may do away with himself – he's had an experience poor chap – he lay wounded with a dead Englishman in a shell hole – eight Germans stood looking down on them – and he had to pretend he was dead. One little knows what these soldier have to put up with – and go through. I heard a Tommy say in the tram the other evening – 'We've no hearts now – we're full of electricity – I would rather be shot in the brain box than die for six months in hospital. You've got to go!'

'What is a charge like?' I asked Frank (ROYLI).

'I saw a German coming, and my eyes were sticking out like this – an' I didn't half go at him – they all had their eyes sticking out at that charge!' he replied.

What near shaves men have. L/Cpl Brown (Sherwood Foresters) told me he took a sentry up to relieve a sentry of the 'Northamptons' and as his man was getting into the latter's place – a bullet got the 'Northampton' and killed him. Brown told me his Colonel 'went over' in front of the battalion saying, 'Come on lads, follow me!' – he didn't go 20 yards before he was shot through the head and died. I asked him (Brown), how he was wounded and he said his sentries had no gas gong, and he returned to the Salient to fetch one and as he took it off the standard, to take it to them a bullet got him in the arm – carrying away a huge chunk of flesh, a nice job we've had with it too! I've had a lot to do with this arm and have dressed it myself many times.

We've got a 1st Bat Gordon Highlander – a new man – with a badly fractured arm – not been set – owing to a gashy wound, that is deep and raw with a tube through it – he has a German sniper to thank for that. We've got a 2nd Bat Scots Guard in 'A' – a very nice fellow (one of R Tempest's Corporals) wounded near Ginchy, two days before Roger was – he was most interested to hear I was his Colonel's cousin and continually asks after him – Mapplebeck is his name – he tells me he knew Roskill – the one-legged Scots Guard who used to come here to have his stump dressed.

Coxon has had another operation – his eighth! He asked me if I was coming in for it – and I think was pleased when I said I was. Poor lad – 'I sometimes think my leg will have to come off – but it would be hard times after trying to keep it all these months', he said. 'Me 'arts not "brok", only badly bent!'
    'Never mind lad,' I said. 'We've never fallen out hev we?'
    'No – an' I don't think we ever shall,' he replied gratefully.
    He walked on crutches to the theatre and got up on to the table himself and smiled at me just before Dr Murdock began to drop on the ether. He was soon off – I undid his bandages for Dr Wilkins and got various things he wanted and Sister B and I each held a leg – it was a nasty big gash he made and he took a lump of bone out – the size of a nut (a loose bit) and packed it and stitched it up – we had to turn him on his face in the middle of the performance and Coxon did a certain amount of kicking and quivering and Sister and I had to hold on! Before we strapped him on the stretcher he started to chuckle and smile and sang softly to himself – a relief from the grunting and snorting that went on during the operation and Jones and Quick (orderlies) roared with laughter (so did the Drs) as they carried him off – Coxon chanting as they went – still of course unconscious.

They had an operation for skin grafting – just before Coxon's and I had a terrible amount of washing up to do – gory towels and sheets

38

and macintoshes – gloves – the operation table to clean – floor to sweep etc. – helped by two other nurses – who came in after the operation. I slipped on a long white gown (overall) and set to work and carried the sheets, towels, etc. to the stores.

'You should wear that white gown always, Nurse de T!' said Jones, who I met on the way. 'I like to see you in it. By the way, Coxon is asking for his sweetheart Nurse de T!' he added, laughing and winking his eye at me, and we went into 'A' – the lad had come round and smiled at me – 'What do you think of her?' said Jones.

'She's a good 'un,' murmured Coxon – closing his eyes again.

We have a fearful job with poor little Tait – he moans dreadfully and weeps and sobs at times, it's awful to hear him – he has a 5 inch tube in his wound, 'How are you boy?' I say. 'A bit easier?'

'No, Sister, it wears us out!' (he calls himself us always) – 'Oh the pain, oh my legs! I won't move Sister, it may go from us soon!' His parents were sent for – he's desperately bad – shot through the intestines. He said he hoped his mother wouldn't come – as it would upset her so to see him suffering – she did come and luckily Tait was easier and not moaning. 'I was terrified the pain would begin, Sister, while she was here,' the poor little lad told us. His sheets and draw sheets have to be changed constantly – 'some job'! He can't move himself and the pain is intense when we have to move him to dress his wound, and he pours with perspiration! He cries and groans away and being one of 25 – we can't always be with him – he really ought to go in 'Galloway Ward' where it's quiet – it's one person's job to look after him – it really is! He's only had morphia once.

Wilkie is in 'G' Ward now (skin cases) – she's much attached to 'A' still and comes and gives me a hand. Gunn laughed as she and I made his bed together the other night.

'I guess you two would get on well together. I lie and watch the little tiffs the other nurses have sometimes.' And looking up at me he said, 'You're the best tempered girl in the world!' It sounds as if I was blowing my own trumpet, but I like the lad's little remarks, they sink in somehow. Two were watching me working – Whittle and Kent.

Whittle, 'What d'yer think of our nurse? She's a champion – isn't she?' - 'Hail smiling morn,' he greets me with. 'Always smiling ain't yer?'

I was putting olive oil and wool into Whittle's ear – the other night, and I heard from Kent opposite, 'Shall I come an' 'ammer it in with me slipper for you?'

They are funny, during hair cutting and shaving in the ward. We've a Sergeant (Sgt Hoyle), the most good natured fellow you could meet (Lanc Fus). I only have to say 'Sergeant, shave this man today,' and he's at work – bathing and soaping etc. – Kent shouted out the other day, 'I've got enough wool at the back to stuff a cushion I 'ave! I want me 'air cut lad!' They've had manias for shaving off their moustaches – Sister B exclaimed, 'Marshall, what have you done? What a sight you look! I never saw such a lot of men – we haven't a man with a moustache in the Ward!' and sure enough first one and then the other have lately shaved them off.

Marshall (Royal Scots) said, 'It got blowed off, the wind was strrrrong!' One lad's hair is thin on top and he said the draft from the window had blown it off.

'P'raps the swallow will take it for their nests,' suggested one lad, 'and a thin bottom they'll have to their nests!'

Today I'm 'off duty' 2 to 4 – which means I shall have to be back to carry ward tea in – that wretched egg problem – who's 'on an egg?' and who isn't – it keeps altering so and if the diet list hasn't 'gone in', woe betide you. While dishing out tea, bread and butter and eggs etc. – you hear the remarks – 'Nurse, will yer peel ma egg?' from a one-armed Scottie, and 'Will yer do the same for a fellow sufferer of mine next door – who's in the same state?' and I have to put down cans of tea and start 'peeling off egg shell!'

'Look at your sheets lad,' I say to another, as I see yellow egg marks spoiling the look of his clean bed.

'I'm sorry, nurse, the egg was lively and hopped out onto the sheets!' he replies.

'Can you manage your egg Marshall?' I say.

'Yes nurse, I think I can sup it.'

They are messy eaters some of them – Sister B spied a collection of plum stones on the bed – 'If I find plum stones again on your bed – I'll go at you!' she said – she's too amusing to listen to, I laugh over and over again when she's rating the men. Tweedie, busy sweeping the floor – says as a damson rolls before his brush – 'Compris little whizz-bangs? Oui!'

Tweedie is a killing fellow – ridiculous how the word 'compris', goes with him everywhere. His bad 'bomb burst' hand is alright now, but he's got an inflamed eye – I gave him his boric lotion in a round bowl, bigger one than usual – 'I'd as soon have that one,' he said, pointing to the washing basin. 'Anyway, if I don't come back, you'll know I've got drowned! "Compris"?'

We had a dance in the recreation room – the other night, quite sport! It was good to feel one's feet again – some of the men dance well. We've a Canadian (wounded at Thiepval in September) who is a perfect dancer – in fact he teaches dancing and bagged several with me straight off. Now the long evenings have started (October 23rd), we have concerts and I hear there's going to be a cinematograph show, which the boys will enjoy.

I spent a half day in bed, the other day. I felt horribly bad – so sick – don't know why. They tried to make me give up and leave work, but I went on duty and stuck it out till 2 p.m. and had no breakfast or dinner – I was mightily glad it was a half day.

No-one knows how good they all were. Bedford said – 'What's the matter, you look a bit sickly about the face!' and Whittle – 'What's to-do with our nurse – are you not so well?' 'I can see you're bad,' said Coxon – 'If you're going to be poorly, my heart'd brok!'

At last Sister B came in and shouted, 'Traffy! Go to your bed!' and I went too.

The girls tucked me up with a hot water bottle – and no sooner had they left than I heard Sister Woodfin (the senior sister) coming down our little passage – she's a dear and the pick really of them all – 'My poor little Traffy,' she said, 'is she feeling sick, what's the matter?' and her arms were round me and she kissed me and fadded after me no end – four times she came during the afternoon and evening – and sat on my bed and brought me things – she's a topper and I love her.

Little Sister B also came and sat talking on my bed from 9.30 to 10.30 p.m. – 'I've been trying all afternoon to get down to you "Traff", but I've been so busy with Tait!' she said. It must have been something we'd eaten – as several sisters and nurses also were ill and sick!

Anyhow I soon recovered and next morning I was on duty at 8.30. I heard Sister B say when she arrived in the ward for dressings – 'Where is "Traff", oh she's there!' and Sister Woodfin as she passed said, 'I must come and look at you again tonight, "Traffie", you have got a cold!' And she did too, and brought me her hot lemonade – which she refused to drink – as she wanted me to have it.

Sister Yorke-Stephens is a little ripper, too, and constantly comes into my cube at night to 'Kiss me good night' as she calls it, and bounces in and sits on my bed – 'Goodnight darlings!' she says – they do spoil me between them here. Her hubby came a few days ago – and she had us cube girls in one after the other and introduced us to him. 'This represents the day staff,' she announced to her khaki hubby. There were about six of us 'cubes' who are 'pally' and we get along 'no end' together. Sister Woodfin walked down the ward the other day with her arm through mine.

'You're one of the pets "Traffie" aren't you?' she said.

'There are many, aren't there sister?' I replied.

'No, only a few!' she said squeezing my arm a little as we went. I hope Sister Woodfin won't go to France – she said she was going – I should miss her so.

*   *   *   *   *

At this moment I am senior in 'A' Ward – 2 VAD under me – Nurse Myers (who for the last two months or so has been bracketed to me – in 'A'), has been put into 'C', to do 'special' to Tait, who is frightfully ill – he was moved out of 'A' a week ago, as it's quieter in 'C' for him. Poor boy, he says he wishes he could die – he suffers so. He clutches at our hands and rolls his eyes, it's awful to see him – we 'A' nurses relieve Nurse Myers – sometimes, and of course often go in to see him – as he belongs to us. He is only half conscious at times, thinks Germans are after him all night – 'Sister, there's an imp on ma leg, it's come out of a big gun – yes, it's there!' and the nurse who's 'on', has to chase the imp off! It is sad what they suffer, these boys! And as one said a few days ago – 'All this suffering, and for a shilling a day!'

It's wonderful how they move about – half roll and half pull themselves out of bed. While we turn the mattress and make the bed up fresh for them – and sit on their next door neighbour's bed with a blanket thrown over their shoulders – little Marshall (Royal Scot) who I've mentioned before, and who had a fearful thigh – lacerated and torn open – said to me tonight as we finished making his bed – 'Will I get on to it now? I'm glad the Dr hasn't any brrroken bones to take oot – A'm no a man – only a buddin' youth!'

'Your nose is shiny – you had a good wash?' we remarked as we tucked him up.

'Yea' like a slide on a frrrosty nicht,' he replied. I watched Dr Wilkins slit up a piece of flesh between the two wounds on his thigh (a deep gash) and pack it – 'Did that hurt you lad?' I asked afterwards. 'No so much, nurse, just the frrreezing nipped a bit!' and that's about all you get from these tough fellows. Bradford told me how he got wounded the other evening, as I sat drying and powdering gloves by his side (he's the show 'case', shot through shoulder and out below heart).

'I was carrying ammunition up to the regiment, when I got done – I lay for hours there – and bled – and it ran in a stream and made a pool and the rats came and licked at it and I couldn't move. My pals found me and said, "Can I do anything, lad for you?" – "No, lad", I said and me heart was rattling, "I'm about done"!'

The stretcher bearers found him and carried him to a trolley – and going down he passed his pal (the boy who just before had asked him if he wanted help) – dead. He spent the night in a ward with quantities of other wounded on stretchers – great shells were hurtling away overhead, ours and the Germans' – but they all passed the wood. Bedford said the trolley in front of the one he was on was smashed to atoms and it and its wounded disappeared

43

from sight! It's a wonder the boy's alive – his wound started bleeding again in that wood and he lay there helpless. He's had dead bone removed pretty deep down too – since he's been here, and I shall never forget it – how he bled after it. Five times the wound was plugged and each time it gushed out and saturated pillows and sheets. He collapsed into Sister's arms, and went quite grey and stiff and cold. He's on the mend now and only wants one dressing a day. I do quite a lot of dressings now – including Hood and Gunn – both are fairly big ones and take a long time.

Marshall was killing tonight – thought he'd make his bed himself – he's a little fellow and has a long flannel night shirt on and pink woollen stockings tied up with ribbons. 'A feel like a long walk in the night, I'm in the pink!' (he's only fit to walk two yards – really).

Coxon roared at him, 'A camera, me lad,' he shouted down the ward from his corner – 'You look beautiful.'

'All is no gold that glitters,' was Marshall's reply.

'Walk to the end of the ward,' I said, 'and I'll push you back in the chair.'

'Ah, is it photo-snatching you're after!' said Scottie. 'I think I'll no walk – put me to ma little bed and tuck it in well – I'll do the vanishing trick,' he said, sliding under the sheets – he is very careful of his leg, and the thought of it makes one shudder – poor little fellow. There are such hunks out of it, and so raw! 'Half o' ma leg's in France maybe?' he said to me one day. He has a quaint way of talking.

'Does Nurse M wake you at 5 a.m.?'

'Nurse M has nothing to do with waking me!' he said.

Those wretched eggs, at tea today – there is always something wrong with them – A little hole was picked in Coxon's and a squirt of yolk was looking out – 'What's wrong?' I said.

'He whistled at me,' he replied and I said 'Go back there.' Groans from Gunn. 'What's up?' the other men said, 'Ooooo-oo – bad!!!' was all I heard as I left the ward. Yet another doubtful egg – Burke had – 'The hen that laid this egg – was not in good health!' Another lad will get a small one sometimes – 'Nurse, this hen must have been starved!' he'll say.

I haven't been able to write any of this book for a week or more – never get time – poor little Tait is just the same – moaning and groaning and shouting – with agony. 'I wish I could die', he moans, 'It's got to come sooner or later – oh, me leg, oh I'm hot and sore!'

Burke is a terrible wreck just now – his leg is all inflamed and swollen – he had an operation in the ward yesterday – an injection of morphia first and then ether – which I gave – I was never so astonished as when Dr Wilkins turned to me and said, 'He's off now – take the bottle nurse, and let it drop on the mask – keep it moving about.' The noises he made – yells simply! and after, sang lustily. 'That's right – we're managing capitally!' said Wilkins – looking up from his chopping and cutting into Burke's leg as I stood at the head of the bed dropping ether. 'Let it come quicker – it's quite safe,' he said, 'That's right!' He packed the deep incision and put two big tubes into the wound, how it bled too! Presently he said, 'That will do nurse,' and I removed the mask and helped with the dressing. 'Now you've given your first anaesthetic,' and he beamed on me as he washed his hands – quite in one of his good moods.

Sister B told 'Kirkie' I'd given it. 'Traffy gave it – and kept him under all the time too!' she said. He came round about half an hour afterwards and was in awful pain of course – temperature last night 103.2.

The doctor has been again today – pulled out the tubes and replaced them with new and fairly put him through it! Poor lad – it is most likely he will have to have his leg amputated – I've been hard at it – since 8.30. Burke has to have a great big flannel fomentations – changed every half hour over his dressings.

'Go off this afternoon, Lassie,' said Sister B. 'I can do without you tonight!' she told Sister Woodfin. I was tired out the other night – so much of the work falls on me now. I was round in 'A' kitchen, and Sister Woodfin came up to me. 'Little Traffie, is she tired? Poor little girl,' said she, as an arm slipped round me – also the Commandant came and said, 'You must be very tired – aren't you? I know you two aren't much good!' I enjoy all the work and if I do feel tired sometimes – well, it doesn't matter!

One of my men – 'Gunn' – is going 'potty' we think – his arm is going on well, all the standing-out muscles and raw flesh have receded and he only has one tube in instead of three or four. Every time you pass his bed he catches you to tell you he has something new in the way of ailments! He kept all my men awake last night – wandering about and had Bedford up six times during the night – he shouldn't be there in the morning and gave him his boots and cigarettes! This morning he'd appendicitis and he was paralysed in the legs – his speech was going and when he pulled his ears forward 'they went back with a click!' Last night he got me to feel his face – it was swelled, he said, owing, he thought, to the bandage on his arm being a little too tight – his hand ached and he was 'flushed with cold' (using his own words) – he also had cramp in his stomach and his eyesight was affected – what can you do with such a one? We are getting him shunted as it's bad for the other lads.

Ford (HRR) with a stump – is another who helps to keep them lively at night – he fights, goes through it and talks – they sit in little groups and listen. Burrell – my Canadian said, 'Nurse, you could listen to him for hours (he's in a shell hole). You must keep low – the Germans are only 10 yards from us, stay till dawn! Each man must have five bombs.' They get to a barn and ask what village it is and what troops are there and he shows a gold watch he'd taken from a Bosche – in fact goes through it all again – just lives it. 'Mercy, mercy! No indeed mercy! No take that!'

Coxon held up his leg for inspection the other day – and such a leg, more like a broomstick – with four long incisions like stripes down the front, sides and back. 'Eh! lad – did you go to bed with your spurs on?' – from one. 'Did you get run over by a cab?' from another. 'No boys – the Colonel's canary kicked me!' replied Coxon.

I am wondering who is going to be on at night work next, 'Wilkie' and 'Anderton' come off next week. 'Are you coming on night duty?' my men ask me. 'And will Nurse Wilkins come on days instead of you? She a bit worisome wi' the lads – that's all that ah her – you mustn't leave the ward! It would break our 'earts, wouldn't it?' They are always turning to me – with some want – someone wants something – 'Ask our Nurse!' says one. 'I've never seen her downhearted yet!' 'Best lass in t'hospital!' says a Lancashire lad – Whittle. 'You must come to "A" when on "nights" – you mustn't go out o' yer ward!' It's nice to feel I belong to them so! If I'm away for a night or half a day – they'll give me a welcome. 'How's our nurse?' from one. 'I've missed you, there!' from someone else. 'I'm glad you're back lass!' from Coxon and so on.

Last night before I 'shut up' for the night – I had half an hour to spare – so ironed three pair of cuffs – in my little 'A' kitchen – Coxon followed me in and watched me – 'If you're going out of the ward,' he began, 'me 'art will be proper brok! There'll be tears!' And I really think he meant it (I've seen him weep once when Sister B 'bent' his heart – as he called it). And he continued as he stood watching me at work, 'I'll get that record of yours "Broken Doll", and have the gramophone up to my bed and play it over and over again – I don't know what I shall do, when you're gone!' (and I felt a little squeeze on my elbow).

'Never mind your heart will be only "bent" lad, not "brok",' I said.

'You've brought some lovely records, nurse,' he said, 'some beauties!' – 'If you were the only girl in the world', 'They didn't believe one', 'Broken Doll' and other new ones (chiefly because this lad wanted them). He slipped out into the ward – put on the 'Broken Doll' (for his and my benefit I suppose!) and again returned to continue his ironing lesson! He's a nice lad, and cuts above the others – and I've a very soft place in my heart for him.

'If I go, my heart will be "proper brok" too!' I said to him.

We've had some good concerts lately – and I love them – a professional sang at the last one – and other good singers – and our lads and we nurses joined in the chorus – and the recreation room resounded again! Their beloved 'Broken Doll' was sung – which went well.

Sisters Boulton and Winstanley are on at night now. Sister B comes every night without failing to see me – and last night I was

47

in bed – about 11 o'clock – she pattered up the passage and stopped at my door and creaked it open and stuck her head round. 'Are you awake "Traff"?' and with one big leap she flung herself on my bed – with her arms around my neck – she's an affectionate little body. 'I've come on purpose to see "Traffie" and I shall talk to her,' she replies as the others try and carry her off to her 'night rounds'. Last night she lit on a tin candlestick I'd put on the floor, for want of a better place – and oh the clatter – and we both went off into splutters – in spite of wanting to do things quietly for fear of waking up the other 'cubicles'. She and Sister Woodfin make such a fuss of me – and I love them both. I have Sister Kirkham now in 'A' – till Sister B's month's over (on nights).

I had such a time in the theatre – last Sunday. My man Martin – was the first to be operated on – Sister Woodfin said I was to go in to it – I was the only nurse, Drs Murdock and Wilkins – and two Sisters. It took two hours – after working and cleaning up and helping to slip the poles into the stretcher I followed Martin into 'A' – and helped to get him into a clean shirt while still unconscious. This so far is the biggest operation I've seen – Dr W had about ten artery forceps at work at once – and used 27 instruments! When I returned to the theatre to help tidy and to prepare for the next – Sister Woodfin said, 'Stay on – certainly – for the next operation.' I felt quite honoured – this boy was Gilbert from 'E' Ward and Nurse Fisher was an onlooker (her first operation) – that's why Sister wanted me to stay and do the fetching and carrying – his was bone scraping and lasted an hour. So I think I did well three hours in hot air and ether, I can stand it splendid now – and don't mind 'sights' in the least! Gilbert often says, 'Nurse, come and tell me all about it – what was it like – you know – you were there!'

We've been slack just the last week or so – only 15 men in 'A' instead of 24 – it is November, a month today Christmas Day! I hope this expected convoy of 80 will arrive soon and let us get them settled and on the mend before then. I've had some half days – and last week a whole day off. I took one of the girls 'Nurse Blackhurst' home with me. 'Blackie' is one of Sister Woodfin's

48

'pets' (as she calls her favourites!). The boys miss me they say – on my half days.

'Going to leave us?' Whittle said, last time I went away – 'You mustn't go from here – the lads think the world of yer – we'd be in a proper mess without yer!'

Fancy, we've only six men in for meals now in 'A' – it takes me no time now (to what it did) to get them fed! 'Chicken for you today boy!' I say – as I place it in front of one.

'Chicken!' he shouts to the rest of the ward, 'That's the stuff they give 'em! Chicken!'

'Ready for pudding, Coxon – Oh no, I see you're still nibbling,' I said the other day.

'What did you say just now about me nibbling – we're not friends, me 'arts brok – then I ought to have two long ears, no we're not friends.'

'Alright then,' I replied – 'So we're not friends – we've fallen out – Goodbye,' and I turned away to go – just to tease him.

'No, lass – we're the greatest friends – we could fall out!'

'Couldn't we though, I'll just try and make you,' I said. 'Supposing I ruffle up this bed (I'd just made his bed with him) and leave you to straighten it again!'

'It's impossible to bear you any malice – lass,' he replied. 'Me 'art'll be proper brok when I leave here!'

Sister Robertson ('Sister Jock' to us all) showed us a letter she'd got from Williamson, 'I shall never forget Moor Park – you're all the pick of the country and are well worth fighting for!' One does feel gratified by the way they write.

Gemmel (my HLI) has written me many letters – excellent ones they are too.

'When I think of my life at Moor Park, well to say the least – it leaves me cold, but then you were all so good to me that I think I am spoilt – I can only say the cold words "Thanks often", and trust that you will realise my sincerity.'

Gemmell to some people would seem dull – this is the reason I said to him, 'Still waters run deep.'

'The more I think of that sentence of yours,' he writes in one letter, 'the more I feel like coming to attention and saluting you – a worthy and very competent officer. Aye, nurse, "many times and oft" when I was at Moor Park, I'd have given more than the usual rate of "tuppence" for "your" thoughts – you were apparently very unconcerned as to what was taking place around you – but nurse, I often doubted this, and still think you could tell some queer and interesting tales about quite a "lot" – d'yer' understand – now don't think I'm attempting to judge you – or mean any harm – as a matter of fact the "still waters" business is a thing I respect.'

I could go on writing yards of Gemmell's letters – they are nearly always three-sheeters. It's the case of living up to the sentence 'Still waters' ... as one must keep one's place, and them in their places 'Compris?' (as Tweedie would say). They try and make love to you – and they do it so nicely it's a job sometimes! 'Nurse, I wish I was an RC to come in the "break" with you – to sit near you!' said Powell (F Ward) – 'Nurse, three days after I've gone I'll bet you get a letter from me!' A Sergeant in the Leinsters – greeted me one morning on my return – 'Nurse – I've missed you – there! You didn't know how much I loved you!' As the gramophone sings forth – a lad will catch my eye – singing the song with it:

> 'You called me broken doll a year ago,
> You told me I was very nice to know
> You taught me what love was, I thought I knew
> But all that you have taught me is how to love you
> You made me think you loved me in return.
> Don't tell me you were fooling after all –
> For if you go away – you'll be sorry some day
> You left me quite a broken doll!'

I may be pouring out medicine – holding up the glass, measuring it out – and the same lad will be just behind me – the gramophone continues – and the words are caught up near my ear (the verse of 'Broken Doll'):

> 'I wonder why I always sigh the way I do
> And now I seem to find my thoughts, are all of you.'

50

I laugh and hand him his medicine! When I first come on duty – and enter 'A' Ward, and before turning to the 'trolley' – a cheerful 'Good morning!' greets me – and my 'Broken Doll' in his corner at the top end of the ward catches my eye and salutes. 'Always first i'th' ward lass, and the last to go – aren't you?' says Whittle.

They've always so many wants at the last minute – and I like to do all I can for them – I must go up and down that ward hundreds of times – and oh how tired my feet feel sometimes – but 'carry on'! They're worth it, these boys, bless 'em all!

'Nurse, I'd like some Bovril!' 'So would I' – 'And may I have some, and nurse, some toast?' This means we must journey down to the kitchen – and make it for them – other men from the wards I find down there – waiting for various things – 'Hullo nurse, how are you?' – 'What can I do for you – is there anything I can do for you?' and with the assistance of my Tommy friends I manage to make my Bovril and burgers – or whatever it is – and as I pass through 'B' Ward – I heard shouted at me – 'Wish I was in 'A' Ward!' I enter 'A' – and my boys greet 'me and Bovril' with - 'That's right! – Bovril – that's the stuff to give 'em – Bovril.'

'You're starting another moustache,' I says to Cassidy as I plant his steaming mug by his bed.

'Yes, nurse,' exclaims Martin, 'It's the Bovril pushin' it up.'

'No, it ain't, it's 'is toothbrush 'e swallowed this morning!' says another.

Those who go down to fetch suppers – often get tastes from the kitchen staff – 'Nurse, I've been squaring the cook,' said a lad one evening – as I saw him munching a large sandwich with slices of beetroot inbetween! – 'Beetroot – same as the nurses have – vinegar purifies the blood, compris?' he mumbled as he stuffed it down. Another boy will say 'I got a banana, – or – a bit o' "cheekin"' – 'Compris being on cheekin' diet? – Oui!' he answers for himself with a wink. 'A banana! – from the wilds of Jamaica, take its temperature!' sings another lad – as it disappears down his throat – and a large banana skin reposes on his small ashtray to add to the other contributions - paper, ashes, grape skins, orange peel etc. – no matter how often they are emptied they always seem to be full!

51

We've just got 66 new cases from France (Rouen), all 'sitting ones' – the stretcher cases are following in two or three days time. So we are busy once more (December 4th). I told my boys 66 sitting cases were arriving that night.

'Oh!' said Marshall, '66 guaranteed sitters!'

'It's not the season!' answered Coxon.

Funny lads, they are always going on in this amusing way. Four in my ward were sent – with others to guide the motors to the door and keep order when the convoy was arriving.

'Where are you going to stand?' I asked one lad.

'Where the ammunition's thickest!' he replied.

Although all these new boys can walk – some are fairly bad – we've two 'Scottish Borderers' with bad trench feet – a 1/4 Gloucester with a shot back, an RE with a tumour – an RFA with a fractured hand and a little Welshman – with a bullet hole in his arm – (he's in the Welsh Reg) – all his English is picked up while with his regiment and he can't understand all we say to him! These men were in a dirty state when they arrived – but we cleaned them up – Coxon's been a brick in giving them tubs – 'And I've had many a smile to myself,' he told me – 'Especially when washing the little Welshman!'

*   *   *   *   *

General French inspected 7,000 Home Defence men in Miller Park last week – a fine sight, and with the rising ground all round we had a grand view – a place with chairs was reserved for nurses and wounded – an officer came up and saluted us and took us to our places – we were close to the sentries lining the road and the General's saluting post was in front of us. It took an hour or more for him to inspect the lines with all his staff. It was freezing cold and our toes ached again! The men did not wait till the end and some of the nurses went too – 'Blackie', 'Wilkie', 'Spencer' and I stayed and it was worth it. We crossed the road (no one turned us back, a bit of uniform does a lot these days) and we stood just in front of the General's car, he stood chatting to his officers – in fact his staff were buzzing all round. I never saw so many red hats together before. General Bingham was there too and his staff (he's in command of the division (30,000) at Blackpool now), a big fine looking man. General French, I thought was a smart little fellow – with a merry face – he was only a yard or two from us – and seemed in no hurry to start – said the officers were to tell the men how pleased he was with their appearance and that they stood to attention as steadily and well as trained troops – 2,000 regulars lined the route. It was quite a job getting back – we found ourselves marching alongside of various companies and regiments as they were mostly coming barrack way. We nurses were called to attend a fainting woman in the crowd!

We are very busy – now – preparing for Christmas concert (nurses responsible for it) – we're doing a Pierrot troop. I'm to be the man in it, and am singing a duet – with Sister Yorke-Stephen's 'If you were the only girl in the world' – also we are getting up a play called 'Mere man', and so far (we've only had one meeting) I'm to take the part of an American girl in it. The men are to be responsible for a concert to entertain us nurses – one day in Christmas week – there's to be a Christmas tree for the men and various other things.

*   *   *   *   *

I've had a bad knock – sad and bad! my name is down on list as senior nurse in 'F' Ward – two under me! My 'A' !!!! It all belongs to me – and all the lads in it – and they hate me leaving them! My '3rd DG' was quite depressed – 'Me 'art's brok!' I heard an umpty voice repeating to itself, and again he started the 'Broken Doll' song – he kept catching my eye when I came near his corner – 'My lass!' he said. 'My heart's just "brok",' – I told him.

He plays with two brown baby dolls (silly boy!) One's mine – and mother presented another to him for fun – they are delicious dolls – lovely goggly eyes – I roared with laughing. Coxon sitting up in bed – and a small object tucked up as cosy as can be by his side – 'Bless her!' I heard him say, he talks rot and blows the little lady's nose – and looks after her no end – and slaps at others who come and want to take her from him – Why do men get such silly babies in hospital?

53

This morning Coxon was asleep when I went into 'A' – brown baby tucked up close to his fluffy head – another man and I stood together and laughed hard – the new baby has a yellow cap – and a fat face – 'Little Fattie' Coxon calls her! – mine a red cap – a ripping little piccaninny – he had this cuddled up to him in bed with his arms round her.

'My baby's over there!' he said – 'This is yours – my lass, all that's left of her!' (This was after I'd told him I was going to 'F') – 'Well,' he kept murmuring – 'well! are you going?' and oh the doleful face! He would hardly speak of it – he was reading The Rosary Book and found little scraps of poems and lines which he pointed to and handed me the book:

> 'The hours I spent with you dear heart –
> Are like a string of pearls – to me.'

I only laughed, I'm afraid – but I read them all as he gave them to me. 'Silly old loony!' I said – poor lad, I know he thinks a lot of me.

'I hear you're going!' said Bedford. 'It's time for us to go on furlough!' he said to the other lads.

'Are you going lass?' said Whittle – 'You needn't be afraid – they'll tackle you, alreet!' So like a Lancashire lad to say it!

'I'll come and see you,' said Ford and Martin in one breath – 'Down in "F" Ward.'

As I went through 'B' Ward, Stanton called to me, 'Nurse! Oh nurse! I'm sorry, are you leaving "A"? You've been in, ever since I been in the hospital – never mind nurse, I'll come and cheer you up – you hate going don't you?' he said holding my hand tightly under the sheets – all the time – 'Poor old nurse!' I might be going for good the way they carry on – and really I feel I was! – Tonight's my last night in 'A' – we shall be 'brok'.

'Poor Traffy', said Sister Woodfin – 'Last night never mind – it'll only be for a short time, I am sorry you'll be on a month's night duty after that!'

'Yes, and I shall miss all my friends!' I said as I knelt on her hearth rug by her fire with my arms on her knees and my head on her shoulder and her head rubbing and snoodling up to mine and an arm thrown round me.

'Never mind Traff! You can come in here (her room) when on night duty – can't you?'

'I shan't dare,' I said laughingly – 'Myers will be back and she'll hate me near you!' (Myers is awfully jealous of Sister W – used to be a friend but has bored her silly by chasing her about.)

'You won't come to me? You better had!' said Woodfin – Blackie and I are her pets – she's the biggest darling!'

'Oh Traff, I'm sorry you're leaving us!' came from the Sisters' Table at breakfast this morning. This from Sister Kirkham, she's been my sister for the month Sister Boulton's been on 'nights'. Hard luck, Sister B returns tomorrow to 'A' and I leave it! Well I must say a painful good bye to my lads tonight, and then will come some 'F' Ward pages of this book. To return to 'A' for a little – we are full there – the men as I leave it are:

Whittle – N Lancs	Nuds
Paterall – S Staff	Lennon – RFA
Coxon – 3rd Dragoon Guards	Morris – Welsh Rgt
Moor – 7th Gloucester	Dwyer – 2nd Welsh Fus
Douglas – KO Scottish Bs	Martin – North Fusiliers
Wilkinson – 2nd Scots Guards	Lambert – KORL
Burke – Northumberland Fus	Marshall – Royal Scots
Ford – K's R Rifles	Youll – Gordon Hds
Hopley – Sherwood Foresters	Bedford
Hawkins	Aldridge
Pet Officer Warren – HMS *Drake*	Cassey – RFA
Barnwell – K's OS Scottish Borderers	Hood – Suffolk
Cpl Martin – Hants Regt	Wilkinson – RGA
Gary – Buckinghamshire Regt	Cassidy – Royal Canadian Regt
Isherwood	

I've had a hard evening in 'A' – plenty of work and endless beds to make – and dressings to help with too – medicines to give out, and all the temperatures to take – they were full of fun – a pill started rolling – 'Watch it! – two to one on the black horse with a white tail!' exclaimed the boy watching his 'No. 9' on the roll.

Bed pans seemed much in demand – and caused much amuse- ment – poor old Coxon and Bedford were kept on the trot – as fast

55

as they screened up one man, another shouted to them. I found Bedford sitting on a bed rail – close to a screened up bed with a khaki handkerchief tied over his nose – 'Be prepared! Is the Boy Scouts motto!' he said. 'Wait for it boy! Wait for it!' shouted some others.

Sister Woodfin enters to call the roll – it always amuses me when she calls a man's name (some boy who hasn't been up since he came) 'Pte so and so!' – 'Here Sister!' he answers in a bright sharp way, as if he'd just managed to squeeze into the ward, mouth full of supper and breathless to answer the roll. I sometimes look round at such a lad and say (as the roll call continues) 'Are you sure you're there?' He chuckles from under the sheets. Sister passes on to 'D' Ward – an absent Tommy of mine will come gliding in – having been love-making in the kitchen or some such thing – 'Absent from parade!' Will sing out the other boys – this starts their commands and orders once more – and they catch it up, one after the other – 'Left! Left! Left!' – they march one of us up the ward probably armed with a washing basin – 'Halt! Right wheel!' As we turn into the 'A' Kitchen at the end of the long ward – laughing as we go – you must march, as the tune is being whistled for you! They love doing this! 'Halt the Boys! Steady the Greys! and let the Rifles pass!' rings out many a time and I like to hear their lusty voices 'Eyes right! Eyes left!' come the orders – and some clown will add 'Eyes backward bend, eyes back again!' Funny lads – just silly babies they really are. 'Nurse lend one your pen – I've just thought I loved a girl! My 'art's brok' (tries to pull out my hanky to weep on).

'Eh!' shouts a lad – ''E's left a feller in lavatory, 'im as can't walk' (the wretch had been wheeled in there – and forgotten). 'Have you any wind, I want to blow up this 'ere air cushion.' 'Don't blow it up like a lifebelt!' Shouts from an unhappy boy – he shot into bed to find a sprig of holly had been put inside – 'Who's done this?' he yells – (no pity from the others) 'Oh,' they say – ''olly, that's the stuff to give 'em, 'olly!'

Whittle returns from Church (it's Sunday, and comes and plants himself by me as I'm talking to Coxon). 'I was a proper unbeliever nurse – before the war and now I go to church, and I pray,' he says.

56

'I said one for you – tonight, and it was a good one an' all! Parson came when I was bad, soon after I'd been wounded and said, "Shall I say some prayers?" an' I said "Thou maun as weel!"'

Roars from Coxon – 'Your language, ducky!' at which poor Whittle said in a hurt voice, 'It's just as I talk – a fella can't help it, I'd a rougher home than thou 'ad.'

'Never mind Whittle lad,' I say – 'You're Lancashire – so am I!'

'Do you know?' says a Canadian (Silver by name), 'Whittle talks like this – "Thee and me'll go and play cards or (taking supper list) Tea for thee?"' 'Thee' and 'Thou' sound so funny to anyone not Lancashire I suppose.

It's getting very near closing time – and I spend the last few minutes sitting by Ford and Coxon, the latter's got tight hold of my hand - 'Shall we give her three cheers when she leaves the ward?' says Ford – no reply from the '3rd DG' – so mopey is he! I get up and get the stick to put out the lights – one by one.

'Good night all of you and goodbye!' I say.

'You hate going, don't you nurse,' says somebody.

'Of course I do you all belong to me,' I say.

'Don't say goodbye,' says my 'brok' lad.

'All right,' I say, 'I'll be coming to see you tomorrow, I'll come and look you up!'

'Have you said goodbye to them?' asks Stanton as I go through 'B'.

'Yes,' I say going up to him – 'My heart's brok!' I've got a sore eye, don't know what's wrong.

'Nurse, what's wrong with your eye?' continues Stanton. 'Have you been weeping 'cos you've left them?'

'I've not been crying lad,' I say, 'but my eye's not right!' I go and get my supper and join the other nurses.

'Oh, of course, she's said goodbye!' they exclaim. Bryning is on night duty in 'A' and laughing I say, 'Goodnight Bryning give my love to "A".'

'Goodnight,' she answers – with a chuckle, 'I know, alright!'

Here I am in bed with a truly awful eye. I had two days in 'F' and got along well enough (but no dressings – made it slow) rubbings galore and special diets and that class of thing. The second day –

my eye was worse – Woodfin came to me – 'Traffy, your eye is bad, you are to go off duty – come along into Matron with me,' and taking me by the hand she took me into Matron's room.

'Yes go off, and foment it, and Dr Murdock will see it!'

Well, she saw it twice and Dr Healy twice, and both said it was very bad – severe conjunctivitis – and that I must have got some septic poison from the bad wounds or dirty dressing in 'A' Ward. My eye was black, red and blue – all swelled up and looked inside out like a bloodhound's! All the white of the eye was fiery scarlet and it ached like toothache. Dear old Woodfin has been a brick – in and out of my cube – putting on fomentations and squirting in black drops; oh how she and I laughed over those drops! I always look forward to her step coming down the passage – 'Poor little Traff!' she'll say, if she's left me for long – 'I have neglected you! When did you have a fomentation on last?' and she'll scurry round and do it for me and bandage me up.

My cube has been a 'dump' once more for sisters and nurses! When the day ones ceased the night staff began their enquiries! And my 'A' men sent up messages to me. 'Tell Nurse de Trafford I went to 'F' Ward to try and find her seven times yesterday!' came from one. 'Stanton ("B" Ward) is inquiring after you.' Bryning enters – 'Coxon's heart is brok – he hopes you better and so on.'

Christmas

I've been off four days and go home for a week, returning Christmas Day! Our sale – including men's own work fetched £100 – it was my first appearance with my eye bandaged – I was besieged by the lads – asking how I was. 'Hullo nurse, have you been wounded?' Whittle said. 'How's our lass, what a pity about your eye – an' such a good lass too!' Dr Wilkins came and said he'd missed me in the ward ('A') – 'Oh yes,' I said, 'I've gone down to "F".' He seemed quite concerned about my eye. Dear old Woodfin, she came down to the station with me.

Well I've had a week's holiday and returned with two eyes instead of one! I got back on Christmas Day to hear what news I expected. 'You're on the list for night duty.' Old Woodfin was one of the first to welcome me back – 'We're glad to see you "Traffy" – we've missed you,' she said throwing an arm round my neck and pulling my hand down on her shoulder – as she so often does and stroking my face.

There was a big Christmas Tree that night – a beauty – and presents for 200 men and nurses, we each went up as our names were called – and Matron gave them out as they were cut off the tree by Woodfin and Winstanley and then we had games to keep the men amused, quite a gay party! Oh, the mistletoe that evening! We nurses couldn't avoid it – it seemed to bristle overhead wherever one stood for a second and where there was none – a bit was produced from a Tommy's pocket! Such a night to come on duty.

'A' was very glad I'd come back to them and showed it in more ways than one! 'That's our nurse!' I heard, as I opened 'A' door at 8.30 p.m. and took over – 'My nurse – my dear nurse come back,' said Coxon – stretching out his arm from his bed and gripping my hand and holding it a long time as I sat down by him. After some time he smiled at me, said – 'I'll go to sleep now'.

Spencer and I am on 'night duty' – I have 'B', 'C' and 'A' Wards and at times 'D'. She has 'E', 'F', 'G' and 'H' – there are two sisters, one her end – one mine and a few VAD – all of whom have not passed their exams – but they can fetch and carry, help with the bedmaking etc. – Spencer and I take temperatures, do fomentations, renew bandages, do up splints, help with dressings and sit up and stay with men who've had recent operations and a nice job we have when they are sick all night from the effects of ether!

Now to describe a night's work. Supper (or rather our breakfast) at 8.30 p.m. with the other girls – then we two 'night birds' clear table and wash up in kitchen – at the present old Woodfin has a wonderful longing for my society! and is always looking out for me, as I pass the Sisters' room and she slips out and catches me and off we go to the Matron's sitting room (empty at this hour) or some such isolated spot. It's a marvellous affection (never met it before).

'Little Traffie,' she says, kissing me – 'I hate you being on night duty, I never see you – it's rotten! Look here, come to my room, will you, later on?' and with many kisses and strokes and huggings

I leave her – how long will it last? She quite chases me and Spencer is highly amused – if she finds us hobnobbing she leaves us – 'two's company' sort o' thing! And for 'Sister' too, to strike up such a friendship! I love old Woodfin better than anyone in the hospital and I'm too glad to be 'the one' for her!

Well, having finished with her for the time being – I go into 'A' Ward – soft shoes and flashlight. All is dark except for a night light burning on the dresser at the end of the ward – voices greet me from the various beds – 'Well lads, how are you all?' (as I go up to different ones). I turn on my flash on the worst cases and ask what sort of a day they've had – 'Oh, it's bad nurse, oh ma leg!' says our 'Scottie' and Dwyer, my Welsh Fusilier, I find in agonies. I move his great helpless leg into a more comfortable position and place it on a pillow and arrange the cage over it afresh.

'Nurse? Shall you bring us some hot milk?' says a voice in the darkness.

'Bovril for me nurse!' says a boy a little further on – with a roguish, merry face, as he peeps out at me from under the blankets. I take no notice at first – and presently 'Martin' tries again – 'Bovril please, p l e a s e!'

I'm their nurse so they try me again – 'I believe I spoil you men,' I say as I carry Ford (KRR) his hot milk – 'No, you don't,' he says. 'Is that hot milk you've brought – well you're a toff – you're a lady!' 'Nurse, will you boil two eggs for ma brrreakfast – I have some in ma locker,' says 'Scottie'. My good old lad Whittle props himself up in bed – 'Eh, do you see our lass – bonniest lass i' the hospital – how art 'er?' he says laughing.

'Alreete,' I answer to please him.

'Do you hear our lass speaking Lancashire!' he says and he looks at me happily and says as he so often does - 'God bless!'

It's queer – these nights give them half to three-quarters of an hour to settle off to sleep and then all is very quiet – just their heavy breathing and restless movements of the few who can't sleep.

Up and down I go – watching them all and ready at the least call of 'Nurse, me bandage is loose!' or 'Nurse, I can't sleep!' 'Nurse move me leg a bit!' 'Nurse, me splint, it's hurting – would you undo it – I'll show you where it hurts.' This is an awful undertaking – those big St Thomas' splints – to undo and fix up again – requiring two or three roller bandages, padding with cotton wool and 'goose splinting' – and lint to prevent fraying the skin – by the iron framework and all this at a time when 1 a.m. dinner is ready, or when someone else demands your attention – Cassidy – a Canadian had to have this done the other night – but I put it all up again by the light of my flash in due time – the skin was rubbed raw where pressure had been and I was pleased I'd taken the trouble – it was a long job.

Then Youll (1st Gordons) has been a job – dead bone removed from his arm – poor boy – all night he was terribly sick – from the ether and hardly slept a wink – I was with him most of the first night after the operation – such a nice fellow and as hard and tough as anything – I was sorry to see him in such a plight. I had to take his splint off at 4 a.m. one morning and rub his arm – it ached and was stiff he said – 'Yes, nurse, that's much better,' he said gratefully to me when I'd finished – many are the jobs we have to do!

I started with Sister Hudson, my end of the hospital and Spencer had 'Tiny'. Then Sister 'Jock' came on – in my wards and Yorke Stephens in Spencer's. 'Stevie' and 'Jock' (we call them this to their faces which shows their popularity) are toppers and ripping to us girls.

At 11 p.m. to 1 a.m., I am relieving in Galloway and 'B' Wards – this suits me and Sister Boulton's bedroom is out of Galloway Ward and I sit and chat with the little lady and go for a wander round the wards now and then – there are not so many wants as in 'A' – only occasional drinks of tea or hot milk and aspirins to give the men who've headaches and can't sleep – little Boulton will say – 'Where are you going Traff?' as I make a move – 'Oh, Malster wants tea', or 'Tait' or 'Bradshaw' in Galloway want some – 'Oh – tea! – bring me some "Traff", there's a dear.' So away to the kitchen and busy at tea-making for the next hour.

At one o'clock I return to 'A' to have a look round (very often accompanied by the Sister) and then off to dinner – that finished, back to 'A' to make another round – the men are often talking in their sleep by that time.

Ford sometimes whistles and drones out songs with no tune to them, time after time repeating the same bar, sort of no ending to them. Youll sat up (opposite bed) – 'Eh,' he said, 'Ford's going to lay an egg!' His next door neighbour, the great Coxon, began to wake up – knitted his brows, blinked, looked at the muttering chuckling Ford and layed on to him with a slipper – 'Stop it!' he shouted, 'do you hear – your noise – ducky! Can't you let a feller sleep!' Bang, bang, went the shoe and the noise ceased for a bit.

They go through fighting in their sleep often – I sat at the end of Ford's bed a few nights ago – 'Shan't go!' he muttered – 'No, shan't go – let another platoon go up – I'm going on digging d- – the REs, let them carry their own stuff up.'

'Ford's in that same old communication trench,' chuckled Youll from over the way – 'He often dreams about it!'

'D' Ward is the one to listen to for talking in their sleep – I've heard three going at it at once – one seems to start others and we had to wake one the other night – he was being badly shelled – 'Where did that one go? They'll be on us next! Keep low – d'ye want your blooming head knocked off – cos I don't! There that officer's hit! – Where do they get their shells from, they must get it out of the ground!'

Then another started – 'Now men, you stick to your points, you'll be alright! Alright! Sergeant, you blockhead – you ignorant puppy, you're just like a ship in distress – ship in – d-i-s-t-r-e-s-s-!'

And that's the way they carry on – poor beggars – sometimes when you're bending over them they'll wake up and cry out with fear and jump and twitch all over – 'It's alright, nurse, I know it's you – I can't help it,' said a Coldstream Guard to me – and he calmed down in a few minutes and settled down again. Poor boys.

We night birds have two hours off duty, generally from 2 a.m. to 4 a.m. – being the quietest time – during this time we get a sleep and curl up, one on the sofa and the other in an easy chair, feet on another, in our 'nurses' sitting room'. Daren't go down to our cubes for fear of disturbing the other girls – at 4 a.m. we are rung up – and sleepy and 'dead to the world' we put on caps and aprons again and sally forth – 4 a.m. is an awful hour – but we get some tea on our way in the kitchen and feel awake again by the time we reach our wards. 5 a.m. we light up and carry washing water to those who can't get up – then we have to drum at the boys and wake them up – I hate doing this – with the flaring light in their eyes they sleep on – 'Good morning,' I say, as loudly as I can and shake at each lad – and before I've gone half way up the ward they are asleep again.

'Here, you, Burke, wake up! Sister will be here directly to dress your leg!' (Grunts from the latter). Then a lively lad will assist one – holding a pillow over Douglas, on high, he brought it down with a whack – 'Hey! You wake up.' This had some effect! 'What's the time?' said one. 'Time you were dead!' said a man smothering his head again under the bedclothes.

Isherwood – has a squeaker – sort of balloon he blows out and he lets it off and the awful squawking that carries down the ward reminds them the wrench of waking has begun. I take Coxon his Bovril he has first thing and lift up his sheets. He is like a baby I always think – arms all folded up – I just take hold of one of his hands – he stirs, opens one eye – sees who it is, and catches my hand in both his and squeezes it tight. 'My lass!' he murmurs. He and Paterall (S Staffs) are great helps to me and do all the sweeping and getting up the breakfast at 6 a.m.

I sterilize instruments at 5 a.m., and sister comes in for dressings at 5.30 – then there are endless beds to make – all temperatures and pulses and respirations for those on four hourly charts – one morning I'd five bandages to put on afresh – the day before's dressings had slipped during the night. A man with a raw stump wanted a fresh eusol dressing putting on – Sister Hudson (lazy little beggar) wouldn't do it for him – so I went to the rescue – it was all sticking and horrid and I managed it when Sister H was out of the way. 'Our nurse!' he said, 'She's my nurse, pick o' the whole bunch!'

These dark January mornings! It's no use putting lights out till we go off duty at 8 a.m. – the hours, 4, 5, 6 and 7 might be in the middle of the night. 'What sort of a morning is it?' I heard a man say to another – 'Strike a match lad,' he announced 'and see!'

63

'Nurse do this for me!' 'Nurse get me that please?' 'Nurse I want ... something.' 'Nurse, please fetch me this and that.'

'There you are – now are you satisfied?' I say as I fetch and carry for them – laughing at their wants. 'You never fail us, Nurse!' – 'Hail smiling morn!'

'I may fall out with you some day,' I say – 'So look out!'

'It would be a falling with the hospital before I'd fall out with you!' shouts Burke.

'There! What did I tell you!' says Whittle from the doorway winking and chuckling merrily as he's busily sweeping the ward – 'The lads here think the world of you!' I heard Isherwood's voice at the other end of the ward remarking – 'Nurse de Trafford! She'd lick the heads off any of the others' (not a very elegant way of explaining himself) – but old Coxon heard it.

'Did you hear what he said? He's right – she can lick the others' heads off – my lass! My chest grew two inches bigger when I heard him say that of you.'

'Don't be silly Coxon,' I said as I smiled at him and moved on to another job.

I didn't think some years ago while dancing some New Year in – that I should be seeing an old year die out attired in grey frock, apron and cap, creeping about in soft shoes (armed with a flash-light) – up and down these wards – well that's how I spent this New Year's Eve. There was a midnight service for those who wanted to go – in the recreation room. Most of the nurses and lots of the men went down – my old Woodfin met me and said – 'We shall come out of church immediately after 12. "Traffy," come to my room, will you?'

I was on duty in 'D' Ward – sitting talking to Dando, who was not in a sleeping mood – when all the mill hooters started screech-ing and buglers from the barracks came up to the hospital and sounded 'Last Post' – lights out for the dying year – Dando and I gripped hands and cheerily wished our first 'Happy New Year's!'

They all came flying up from church soon after that – Coxon was well in front and tore round into 'A' Kitchen to be the first to greet me. 'A very happy New Year – of the very best!' he said – catching

64

hold of my hands and squashing them tight. I was soon surrounded with the other lads – they were all so happy and bright – it was a pleasure to be amongst them all. Sister Woodfin came all the way up to 'A' to find me, with her best wishes, sweet of her coming all that long way – at that hour 12.15! It was a long time before we got the boys to bed (we night nurses). Off duty at 8.30 a.m., I got to the 9.30 Mass at the English Martyrs and made my way to our digs – found Spencer had already arrived and spent a happy New Year's Day in bed!

'D' wing this time on 'nights', we've been busy rehearsing for the play 'Mere Man' and also the Pierrot Troop – there are 17 of us in the latter and we have great fun, – 6 to 8 p.m. and then shuffled into our nurses' dress and went straight on night duty (i.e. 'Spencer' and I) – most of our songs were choruses – one following the other (except for a few solos) and recitations and a duet 'If you were the only girl in the world' that 'Stevie' and I sang – and then we had a minuet danced by 'Anderton', 'Spencer', 'Dorothy' and myself. We paraded through the wards afterwards, to let the men who couldn't be taken down, see us. Matron also held a reception for us Pierrots and Pierrottes – and we trooped into her room and she beamed on me quite graciously in my Pierrot trousers, frills and poms.

Spencer and I have stuck this night work well. We've had no big convoys arriving in the night mercifully – only one small one of 15 and only 2 men were sent up into 'A' Ward – that was the night of our staff dance – so we scurried our new ones into bed and returned to our dancing!

One evening I entered 'A' at 8.30 and went tip-toeing round the different beds with my flash, when a little whine came from the corner bed – 'Me 'art's brok' it piped. 'Have you heard' (clutching at my hand as I went up to him) 'I'm going! Me 'art's brok and I am proper poorly, me 'art's like three black puddings – Goodbye lass – wait for it!' and he snoodled under the bedclothes.

I wasn't surprised as I knew he was 'marked out'. Over a year in one hospital is too much for any man and a change will I hope do him good. I shall miss the boy – he's always jealous of 'his nurse'.

I was sitting between Coxon and an 'F' Ward man during a 'men dance'.

'Come back to "F"!' one said.

'I'm in "A" on night duty now,' I replied.

'Leave "A" and return to us!' he said.

'Look here, me lad,' said Coxon – 'Remember there's an "A" man sitting next to you – so be careful!'

Well we've nearly done our time on 'nights' – and come off at the end of the week – I wonder if I shall get back into 'A' on days or be shifted to a new ward – a few more nights to flap about in felt shoes (red ones at that, with nice camel's-hair stuff lining and turning over on to the red). 'Bon' shoes' the men call them.

Funny boys, they start jabbing their little teasing remarks at each other – and roaring with laughter and fun as soon as they are properly awake! 'Hullo, Ham and Eggs,' they shout to the man who (not always willingly) turns out of bed earlier than the others to go down to the kitchen to push up the breakfast trolley. (Ham and Eggs', such a name!) 'Any buckshee eggs this morning?' they ask him. 'That egg is just beginning to make itself heard!' 'Oh no – it's not – it's fresh! New laid! Straight from the hen,' is the last remark I hear, as I rush on with my temperatures.

'You're down this morning,' I say as I chart 97.4 – a comical wink comes from a boyish face snuggled into the pillows.

'There's many a man dies going down!' he adds.

Another lad sees his chart marked the same for the last four or five times and says to his next door neighbour as I hang up the chart, 'That's the line to keep . . . a nice straight line o' trench!' I've been advancing other replies – 'Mine is returning steadily' says a third boy. 'Nurse,' shouts another. 'Give me the egg boiler'. (Egg boilers being one of their names for thermometers.)

'Scottie', our little Royal Scot, was asleep the other morning and I found the other lads had tied artificial flowers on to his bed rail and put some in his hand and had written big cards – which reposed on his chest. 'Marshall, Royal Scot, killed in action from the effect of a No. 9 pill'. I left him still lying in when I went off duty.

Roars of laughter from several boys – who stood admiring a tall fellow in a wee grey jacket – sizes too small for him. 'Eh, lad give the little boy 'is coat back!' they jeer at him – they poke fun where there is the least excuse for it. I scurry on with what fomentations there are to do – and clap a steaming hot one on to some lad's wound,

'Can you stand it?' I say.

'Eigh, let it go on,' and after holding his breath a moment he remarks without so much as a smile looking up at me – 'Summer's coming!' (his way of saying it's a hot one!).

Old Quick (orderly) and I get on with bedmaking – one after the other! One after the other! Till we go on mechanically. Presently he straightens his aching back and looks dryly at the wounded laddie in the bed – 'If you hadn't gone to please the King, we shouldn't have been doing this!' he remarks.

Well it's come to an end (our 'night work'). 'Spence' and I left at 8.30 – at least left the Wards then – I had a letter from a girl saying if I was sick of nursing would I go to a Catholic Hut – a sort of canteen – reading room place, and help with that – I must pay 15/- a week towards board and washing. I read this to 'Spence' in the sitting room before we left for our 'sleeping digs' and for fun said – 'I think I'll go!'

A muffled voice came from Woodfin's bedroom, 'Traffy! You'll do no such thing!' Suppose she really thought I was in earnest and was determined to nip it in the bud. I should hate it after all the bother of learning what I have, too! No thanks!

It amused Spence and myself! We were rather undecided about taking a message that last morning when leaving the hospital and passed and re-passed 'A' windows three or four times. Youll, my 1st Gordon, stuck his head out of one of the windows and said – 'Spin a coin, to decide which it's to be!' (rather to the point, I thought). I've got two nights and one day at home by way of a rest when coming off nights! Where shall I be on returning I wonder, what ward?

*   *   *   *   *

.

I'm back again – working away on 'days', and it's a change for the better I must say! Sister Boulton I met in 'B', as I entered the hospital – on my return – 'Hullo, Sister, what ward am I in?' I greet her with.

'A,' she says, beaming at me. 'That's right!'

I say, 'I'm glad,' and in a whisper she adds:

'I asked for you – I told Matron I wanted you!'

The boys in 'A' were very glad to get me back and all said some nice little things by the way of a welcome. 'Come back to us? Our lass! God Bless!' broke out Whittle in his same old words he uses so often. He's so genuine – true as steel and one of the best men in hospital.

Found Coxon was still lingering on – under orders to go to Blackpool Convalescent Hospital – or rather Camp – he'll never stand it.

Two days after I returned to 'A' on day work he left. Bedford and Whittle carried his kit bags and saw him to the gate – he was quite overcome, poor laddie. Whittle said afterwards, 'It was not the fact of going, but the "goodbyes" that broke his heart.' Martin (North Fusiliers) has Coxon's corner now, there was keen competition for it.

The first thing of importance to happen in the way of operations was Taylor's (2nd Gordon) and I was the 'A' nurse present at it – it was quite a serious one – lasting two and a half hours – the first real internal one I've seen – and such an incision they made! It was for hernia and took much longer than the Drs expected – rather a complicated case – an extraordinary interesting one, and I was kept very busy in the theatre cleaning up, and sterilising about 30 instruments after it was over. I love theatre work and know my way about well and where to lay hands on things when asked for in a hurry – it wants a bit of knowing too.

To fly from one subject to another – our concert (Pierrots) for visitors and our relations and friends – had been fixed for Thursday, February 1st, it ought to have been followed by the play 'Mere Man' – this we had to knock off because the very day, or rather night, before, a convoy of 92 men from France arrived –

practically every one a stretcher case! 'B' is now the convalescent ward (the 'A' Sister has charge of it). Sister Jock and her nurses now staff 'H' Ward and it was filled with men of this convoy – such a length of a ward, 32 beds and the amount of stocking it required from medical stores!

We in 'A' only took ten new cases in as we were busy with bad cases as it was! They began arriving at 11.00 – and by the time we got them in to bed and Dr W had seen and dressed the most serious cases it was 3.30 a.m.! A proper 'night out'! We were tired – going on duty again at 8.30 a.m. We did dressings till close on dinner time and then were allowed off (Pierrot nurses) as when we got out from first staff dinner – there wasn't enough time for us to dress up in our poms and frills! Then old Woodfin required assisting into her Pierrot things ('some boys' she and I made!)

We were all photographed in a big group before we started the performance – outside, in lovely sunshine – might have been on purpose for us! We had a lot of new songs thrown in this time – I still sang my duet – but with Nurse Cuff instead of Stevie and it and the dance in between the verses went quite well. I believe the effect and grouping was good – (blue dresses, red poms, big white ruffles and frills and little bright red pointed caps poised rather 'chic' on one side of our heads – with white poms on).

Someone in the audience remarked – 'Are these professionals?' 'No,' said one of our lot, 'Why, they are the nurses of the hospital!'

Here is a rough programme –

Opening Chorus – 'Gather round the banner of V. Country',

1. The following choruses sung by the troop
    'Moonlight'
    'A Rose, A Kiss, A Ring'
    'Little Fly!'
    'Sleepy Pyjama Girl' (and dance)
    'Come and Join the Pullman'
    'I've Got a Girl in Pekin'

2. Song and dance –
   'In Your Crinoline, I Love You!
   (by Nurses Powell and Wilkins and chorus by troops)

3. Song
   'A Perfect Day'
   by Nurse Spenser – chorus by troop

4. Song and chorus
   'My Home in Kentucky' by Nurse Holden

5. Recitation – by Nurse Myers

6. Song and dance –
   'If You Were the Only Girl in the World'
   by Nurses Cuff and de Trafford

7. Song – with chorus and dance –
   'Little Girl of Lost Island, I'm Longing for You!'
   by Nurse Holden

8. Choruses by the troop –
   'When I Leave the World Behind'
   'Tennesee'
   'Kentucky' (whistled by troop)
   'Yocahana Girl'
   'My Heart is Calling You'
   'The Old Cocks are Busy Crowing Now the "Bantams"
       Have Gone Away'
   'The Girls We Left Behind'

9. Song –
   'Every Little While'
   by Nurse Spencer – Chorus by Troop

10. Song – by Troop
    'Some Night, Some Waltz, Some Girl!'
    (two couples waltz – Nurses Anderton and Powell and
        Nurses Corothy Toulmen and Taylor)

11. GOD SAVE THE KING
(troop 'to attention' – Pierrots salute as curtain falls)

Not a bad little programme – taking it all through. Well our day was not then finished by a long way – we scuttled back into our nurse's dress – got tea and then back to the wards – wards bristling now with men – we are absolutely full up – even little 'G' and Galloway Wards. We worked 'double time' and were let off at 8 p.m. – as most of us went to the dance at the Guild Hall – given by Matron and Lady Hollins for hospital workers – three taxi loads of us left the hospital together. Old Woodfin got hold of a pinch of my coat, as we stood waiting in the doorway – which decided my taxi for me! And I found myself sitting with Woodfin, Boulton and the new Sister 'Walker'. I keep forgetting Boulton is now 'Sister CB', she married Major Clayton-Barker, RFA just before Christmas.

On arriving we decided to stick to one corner of the ballroom and to have our own sets for the lancers. Millions of nurses were there – and ambulance men – but they made no difference to us at all. We six girls and three 'Sisters' – and two very lively RFA officers – Capt Thompson and MR Adams – both great sports and full of go – they danced with our little lot all night and we'd great fun, when we hadn't the officers we danced with each other. Capt T and I hit it off well together, how many did we dance? He heard the girls and Sisters calling me 'Traffy' every minute and soon began himself! Woodfin was highly amused – 'I heard the Captain,' she said 'every time I came near you, Traffy! "Traffy" he kept mumbling as you danced.'

Old Woodfin is a sport and enjoyed herself as much as anyone of us – she heard these two boys wanted to take us home – and continued to pack the other taxi loads (herself going with them) so as to leave 'Wilkie' and 'Adams', 'Thompson' and me to follow in their taxi. It was 'Some night, some waltz,' as the song goes – good to feel one's dancing toes again. What with the convoy arriving, the Pierrot concert, then a ball on top – we were not as fresh as we might have been – still we enjoyed ourselves, no end!

The following morning – I was busy in the ward – a message was brought – 'You are wanted on the telephone.' Off I

71

dashed to Matron's office – (such a nuisance the thing being there!).

I lifted the receiver to hear a familiar voice, 'Is that Nurse "Traffy"? It's Captain Thompson speaking.'

Matron sat glued to her desk just underneath the telephone – and I did as much talking as I dared right over her back – why can't people have the nous to get up and leave on these occasions? – I couldn't say to him, 'Shut up – Matron's here!'

Now to another subject – we had a small fire by way of a change in the cube sitting room – Woodfin was not feeling well and as usual I was in her room – it would be about 10.30 p.m. Presently Spencer shouted 'Girls! Come at once. Come quickly – there's a fire!'

Out of bed hopped old Woodfin in her pyjamas and we flew into the room – and other girls had come in from their cubicles – a piece of asbestos behind the gas stove had set alight – the pipe running upright at the back had got very hot – anyhow flames had begun to lick up the wall – and those wooden buildings would burn mighty fast if properly got going. 'Spence' was dragging the 'fire queen' off its stand in the corner – luckily we had one! and Woodfin seized it – turned it upside down and turned it full force on to the flames – the roar of splashing, rushing water could be heard in 'E' Ward! All was well – and we soon got it out – a bad job if nobody had been in the sitting room at the time it started.

It's nothing to write about, but it will bring a funny little picture back to my mind when reading this book of 'Life of a VAD' – how we all stood watching old Woodfin capering about armed with a heavy 'fire queen' – in her stripy 'pyjamas' and hair in pins – when a moment before she was feeling ill and rotten in bed – never mind Woodfin to the rescue!

We've got a good many Scots boys in this new convoy – nice laddies they seem. Gordons, Camerons, Argyle & S Hds, Black Watch, Royal Scots, etc. We've got a nice fellow, a (1st) Coldstreamer – out of H. De T's company – named Middleton – seemed pleased he'd got his Captain's cousin as a nurse – we've moved three of our old men into 'B' and been sent three very serious cases out of Galloway. One with gangrene toes – one with a swollen foot, tubes in three places – and four deep incisions on his instep all packed with gauze – it will in all probabilities have to be amputated – and the third man has had pneumonia. The last two are on special diets – food every half hour and brandy every three hours – it all adds very much to our already busy ward.

I held the gangrene toe man's leg while his dressing was done – his first night in 'A' Ward (Preston his name is) – a pluckier man you couldn't wish for with a bright face. It reminded me of dressing a sheep for footrot. I had to hold on hard and fast – he twitched, writhed and jumped so in sheer agony – as the scalding strips of lint were drawn in between his toes, (and such toes) all dead – nearly hanging off – and a raw bleeding ring round the base of each which showed the live flesh from the dead – a most repulsive looking sight. When his toes are ready they will be amputated and I hope, his foot saved.

A poor Scots lad died a few days ago – Pte McCord – he was one of the new 'H' Ward men, and through the effects of a leg wound he started to haemorrhage badly one night – 'Sisters' rushed from all parts and they arrested it – only to start again the next day. We had just come out of first staff dinner – when the news was brought – and I saw Sister Jock running down that long passage to 'H', as she's never run before! Someone rushed to the telephone to try to get Dr – anyone – our own were all out it seemed. Woodfin dashed to the theatre, got Easterly (an 'H' nurse) and came for me as a second – we worked like troopers to get the theatre ready, bowls and lotions out – blankets on the table, instruments sterilised, macintoshes out and doctor's coats and unfastened the big 'drums' with the sterile swabs and dressing materials in and all the silk worm gut and needles – even had the huge oxygen apparatus if required (it reminds me of a hideous and enormous shell that might explode at any minute!).

Dr Collinson arrived and Dr Sellers heard we'd been telephoning for him and rushed to the hospital in time to assist Dr C – also Dr Murdock arrived to give the anaesthetic. I shall never forget that operation – the poor lad, bleeding to death except for the tourniquet that was turning his leg black and blue – was brought in on a stretcher. White as death he looked – his big long-lashed dark eyes and hair making him look paler still – he clasped his white hands over his head when we laid him on the table – 'Oh, come awa' Doctor – come quiet,' he kept saying – he was in such a weak state, a whiff or two of ether and he was off – they never thought he would have lived during that operation – his pulse was shocking and colour grey, blue and awful – they couldn't give chloroform and only enough ether just to keep him under.

For two solid hours those Doctors worked – slashed and cut at his leg to find the femoral artery – and ligature it, they let the tourniquet loose to try it – and blood streamed, as I could never have believed (or anyone else who hadn't already seen a spouting artery), it shot from his leg clear over the table – on to the floor, and from such a height it sounded like water being poured out of a watering can on to the oilcloth floor! They tightened up the tourniquet again and stitched him up – and would have taken his leg off – if he could have stood it. He was too far gone and weak – they carried him out (tourniquet still on). They told me he was the life of the ward when he first came in to 'H' – they were so fond of him – and what a plight he was in then. Poor lad he'd run three miles after being shot – doesn't it sound cruel!

No one in the theatre can conceive the mess of the place – perhaps from my description though, they can to some extent – and oh, the saturated gooey sheets – and macintoshes – a great deal of it fell to me – the wringing out, and wiping up – as Easterly naturally went to 'H' with the boy.

Wilkie who like me enjoys the theatre came in from 'A' – and gave me a helping hand – Woodfin worked like a Trojan too – and squeezed and wrung out those messy sheets alongside of me.

'Well, Traffy, I don't suppose you ever thought some years ago that you'd be doing this!' she laughed.

'No, I can't say I did!' I replied as (with Dr's White slip on from my chin to my toes) I kneaded away at those sheets in the sink.

McCord lived all that night – and I went to 'H' to see him the next day – he looked very, very weak and pale – his people had to come from Ayrshire and were to travel all that night –

74

they arrived at 6 a.m. – not to see their boy as he died at 11 p.m.

'Laddie,' said his nurses – 'If you should be asleep when your people come, is there any message you'd like us to give them?'

'I'm A1.'

Here's a bit of Scotch grit for you – and an example of what our Tommies are like – only another, 'done his bit' like thousands of others!

At the present time Wilkie and I run 'A' Ward between us (two under us) and we take it in turns to do the small dressings (about eight of them) as it saves our Sister having to do them and she's got enough with the heavy cases – also it's good for us to do them, and Sister trusts a good deal to us two.

Sister 'CB' has gone on night duty again – this time we've been given Yorke-Stephens as our Sister – and we're glad to have her. She gave Wilkie and I a pat the other day, on leaving the ward – saying in her sweet little way – 'I'm very proud of my little nurses!'

I fancy I've mentioned about Myers – how she chases Woodfin about – she used to be a great pal of hers – but now (and no wonder!) bores her to tears. She won't see, or take hints or snubs from Woodfin – she can be as snubby as she can all day and yet Myers won't see she doesn't want her company – it's enough to drive anyone silly. Be friends, I say, as long as that person wants you – but don't chase – and don't pester that person with your society.

She was daggers drawn with poor little 'Blackie' – just because Woodfin was fond of her and took notice of her – she is so frightfully jealous. Old Woodfin called 'Blackie' and 'Traffie' her two children – long before 'Blackie' went off duty for several months. Well since Woodfin has been deprived of her 'Blackie', 'Traffy' has been 'the one' for her – and it has riled Myers fearfully as Woodfin was constantly calling me into her room – etc. Still Myers pressed herself upon poor old Woodfin – wherever the latter went, Myers pattered after her – if I was in the theatre, in the stores, in Matron's room – anywhere where Woodfin was – Myers was sure to enter! Woodfin would look up at me when she'd gone and say, 'Done it again! Never mind her Traffy, take no notice!'

All the while, I was very nice to Myers, I felt sorry for her – and used to go out with her although she really didn't interest me in the very least! – But I thought it best to keep sweet with her because of Woodfin!

She went at Woodfin one day for allowing us in her room and Woodfin bristled at this and said, 'Hadn't she the right to ask anybody she liked and to have them as long as ever she chose in her room?' Myers is madly in love with 'W' and 'W' does not respond to it! Poor Myers! You can't make a person love you.

The other girls treat W's affection for me as a huge joke – so do I! Often W will go to her room (which is out of the cube sitting room) and leave the door ajar – presently will come a muffled voice – 'Traffy!' The girls sitting round the fire with me will smile – 'Listen! There she is!' They'll say, 'Go on Traffy, she wants you!'

I don't like doing this if Myers is present. I felt she was beginning to hate me, and one day came and wept on my shoulder – a most uncomfy thing for me – 'Why wouldn't W talk to her, she had me for ages with her – would I ask her why it was she never spoke – would I do what I could for her?' and so on.

How I love my old Woodfin – but as for chasing about – and pressing myself on her, no! I wouldn't do it unless I knew she wanted me – and it's good to see she does! We go out together – go to the Empire or the Hippodrome – and why not? Why shouldn't two girls be pally? Myers resents this. One day the bomb fell! I felt it was coming. I wasn't well and had a day or so off duty – Myers wasn't well and remained in her cube which was opposite mine – she was ordered home by Dr Healy – and refused to go flatly – he came in to see me also and said, 'When your temp is down, you go home, too, and get rid of your cold.' When he'd gone Myers suddenly jerked out at me over the way – 'I shan't go, till you do!' Anyhow, Jock came bustling down the passage – and ordered her to pack up and get ready to go; the change would do her good and her mother was coming to take her home in a taxi.

This annoyed Myers exceedingly! I felt this – also Woodfin kept creeping down to see me and bring me little things and hardly put her nose into the 'hurt Myers' cube. I couldn't stand being in the cubes any longer – W offered me her bed to lie on or her fire to sit by – but fearing M would flare up if she knew I'd taken refuge in W's room, I said I'd be alright on the sofa in the cube sitting room.

During her packing (her mother was helping her) she came in to me and stormed – 'You've come between me and Woodfin!'

'Don't talk nonsense!'

'You know you have! Woodfin does it to hurt me and they all say the same!' (They all denied having ever said such a thing.)

I let M say what she wanted – and just felt boiling with rage inside. After she'd gone – old Woodfin returned from town with buns and cakes, and sweets for 'Traffy!' and she didn't do it to hurt Myers – Myers had gone. She was so sweet! – if M had seen her then, she'd have had to alter her opinion of Woodfin's love for me.

Her arm went round me – as she sat on my sofa (I was ill and feeling rotten).

'Poor little Traffy,' she said – 'What's she been saying to you? Will you tell me about it darling? How could she speak to you like that?'

Dear old W, she took her hat off and returned with her glass.

'I'm going to have tea with you, Traffy!' – she said as she took my tea pot and started pouring out into 'glass' and a very nice little tea we had – by that fire and I told her my troubles and she petted me a lot.

'As if you could love a person on purpose to hurt someone else!' I said, laughing – for now I'd Woodfin to protect me, I didn't care!

'No, of course not, Traffy!'

'Then you don't love me because of hurting Myers? You do love me a tiny bit?' I said to tease her.

'Traffy, a tiny bit? No, a very big bit!' said old Woodfin and she means it too. I tell her the first snub she gives me, half as small as the ones she tries to give M – and I've done with her! And we both laughed.

I fancy we had 'flu in the cubes. I went home for a week and stayed a fortnight, awful throat, cough, neuralgia, temperature etc.

– and every day I kept hearing from someone at the hospital that 'Nurse so and so had gone home ill!'

Old Woodfin wrote me ripping letters – 'I wish I could go and nurse you Traffy darling – I'd take such care of you – don't come back till you are fit – although your Woodfin is very lonely, and misses you very much . . . ! Heaps of love,' she ended one letter – and lots more writing for you (and she only does it to hurt someone else? – I don't believe that 'Lady Myers').

*   *   *   *   *

We've had such a lot of good concerts – and really for a fortnight or three weeks after Christmas there was something in that line every evening for the men. We didn't see very much of them as it always means a scurry 'these concert nights' – evening dressings rushed, ward tidied, beds made, men got ready to be down in their beds or lifted into long chairs and wheelchairs of every make and sort.

In many cases the 'practice boards' on the beds are too wide to go through the doors and it means lifting the men out onto other men's beds. Then there's the job of getting them to the recreation room – sometimes the runners on the bed legs come off – especially if a lively lot of convalescent boys assist in the 'great push' of beds! and take them down at a mad gallop! If one meets one of these 'express' beds coming – beware! The weight of the bed – the energy of the men and the pace, carries you along with it – till you gather up courage and hop on one side and let the flying procession pass! Two beds collapsed with men being taken down in this style (one man, Malsten, with an amputated leg). Since then 'No beds allowed down', only men who can be lifted into long chairs. Then there's the rush back to the wards – and the tucking up into bed again. We are always late leaving the wards these nights!

The men have changed so much – some gone to convalescent camps – others back to fight, and the Canadians and New Zealanders and Australians to their own hospitals. Now (March 14th) I am senior in 'A' – Nurses Leigh and Eccles under me – Ford, Whittle, Coxon, Cassidy, Burke, Moor and most of the old boys have left us – good old Youll (1st Gordons) is still with us – and his next door neighbour McDonald (1st Cameron Highlanders) is a very nice Scottie – Wilkinson (Scots Gds) and Middleton (1st Coldstreams) are good sorts, Martin is still in the ward – and the others are Preston – Hall – Hopley – Eaton – Evitt – Hawkins – Evans – Dunhill – Needs – Williams. Forsythe left two days ago.

Yesterday ought to have been a half day for me – but as Sister 'CB' is holidaying, and there were two operations, both in 'A' – Sister Woodfin said it would be far better if I stayed on duty – and a day of it I had! Preston had five toes amputated, and Youll's arm was opened up and humerus scraped, two hours it took for both to be finished (Dr Sellers did them). I was in the theatre for both of them – had a late luncheon with 'Kirkie' and 'Woodfin' – then back to clean the theatre – and then to ward – where two wretched Tommies were asking me, 'Nurse, hold me hand!' – 'You're alright – yes – you're alright,' said a semi-conscious Gordon – as he caught at my hand as I lent over him, from one to the other I went! First to Preston – then to Youll – both were in such agonies we injected morphia – I had a tiring day, as I helped to take an inventory of splints and medical appliances, and tidied shelves with Woodfin in the stores – a terribly muddling job. Then at night (second house) we went to 'Empire Theatre' – Woodfin, Spencer and I – the end of another 'perfect day'!

I've been having drill instruction – and can now 'present arms' – 'slope arms', 'order arms' etc. – the boys are quite proud of their recruit. Picture me armed with a crutch or long broom, standing to attention – while orders are yelled forth!

The men have taken it into their heads to get suppers – twice lately they've brought in tripe. 'Flab' I call it – 'What have you got tonight?' I say, as I look down at a hungry group – seated round the table, which generally has vases of flowers on – 'Oh lord, flab again!' I say as a newspaper is unrolled and a large white quivering mass of tripe is brought forth! Vinegar in a tea cup, besides their (usual) bread and butter, and tea, makes up this rich repast! Tinned lobster was the fashion one evening, and a 'D' Ward man informed one next day that the 'A' men kept them awake shouting in their sleep! I gave them a spread one night – it was the subject of long discussions as to what they should buy – cold pork and pineapple chunks was what they finally decided on!

They've gone quite mad lately – and play like children, how they keep it up I don't know, 'pretending', and acting it all so seriously although no one is looking on (as it happens I often stop working just to watch them) – it amuses one hugely – and in earnest about it – I must try and scribe some of their little side plays. Youll (my Gordon) met me at the ward door – thus – his own Scotch bonnet on – a Gordon silk handkerchief hanging round his waist for a kilt – trousers turned up as high as they'd go – a stiff-bristled brush hanging round him for a sporran – blue socks and Sister B's starchy cuffs on his ankles for spats – and with a rubber hot water bottle tucked under his arm he proceeded to parade up and down the ward – playing the bagpipes – pumping away with his arm – and imitating the wails of that instrument! He and Preston are as light-hearted a pair as you could find anywhere! I found them pushing the trolley (with all the instruments and bottles and syringes jingling as they went), shouting – "'errings, 'errings, bowney 'errings, big as mackerel! – Live cockles! Cod fish! Fresh English tomatoes – fine juice oranges – lemons three a penny!' and so on – bellowing for all they were worth as they went on selling their goods into 'D' Ward.

'For goodness sake – be careful of the trolley,' I flung at them but really, one had to laugh – and when tired of their game they carefully handed it back – safe in its old corner. Another game they love is pretending to be the doctor – and they go at it in a most serious way (stuff and nonsense, of course, the whole time).

'Yes, he's badly,' says my old Gordon – Youll, bending over a lad's bed. 'Let's take his respiration. A probe please!' (an old wooden knitting pin) 'Now then, his temperature' (gets the big ward thermometer that hangs on a hook) and places it between the man's teeth. 'Yes,' he says thoughtfully, 'Say what you have to say – you're breathing your last! He's stopped breathing – he must have passed away!' he adds, turning to the other men who stand round watching.

80

He'll go to another man, 'You want a bowl do you – well, will you be sick if I bring you one?' (turns to fetch one) – 'Now don't be sick, stick to it till I come back!' The bowl is rushed for, head held – a most realistic display of vomitting takes place on the part of the patient – and a reel of cotton is dropped into the bowl with a bang and a rattle. 'There, now you're better,' he says. 'See, nurse (turning to me) he's brought up a bobbin o' cotton!'

'Well, you really are a "potty" lot,' I say laughing. 'What are you coming to!'

Youll looks up at me with a twinkle. 'Nurse,' he says, 'if you let us alone, we'll play for hours!' Cheery beggars they are.

Woodfin came through the other evening when they were kicking up a row – she was only amused. 'What are you doing,' she said, 'selling fish?' She saw them at one of their 'suppers' once. 'What's this for?' she asked. 'Oh, it's an anniversary every night, isn't it – just now!' she said, and left them gobbling their tripe.

I saw a funny performance a night or so ago – I'd been down for a concert rehearsal – and had left my junior in the ward. Youll (as per usual) was the 'star turn'. 'Chippy' (Hawkins) was standing on the table, a sheet held high up (to look like a dressing tent) and Youll emerged from it – trousers and sleeves rolled up – and trying to stick out his muscles and treading with huge steps as if he was a giant – he proceeds up the ward – an iron is placed in the centre of the floor and he pretends to be a heavyweight lifter – pants and struggled and gets down on all fours – and at last raises the iron amidst cheers. 'Good lad, Jimmy – you'll do it – stick to it lad! Bravo!' You'd really think he was lifting 100 tons! This game amused them for ages.

'Chippy! Come off the table,' I say. 'You'll get into a row – you're all making a fearful noise! You'll be reported – I warn you!'

'I don't care now, if the King comes!' replied Chip. They'd got thoroughly wound up.

'You'll be reported,' I continued, bursting with laughter all the time.

'Well, I've been over the top before and I can go over again,' he answered – cheerily, but all the same they sobered down for me.

81

Sister B came in one morning early and saw this exhibition – Youll (of course) pretending to paddle on the seashore – trousers rolled up – bare feet and armed with a red fire bucket – he was wandering up and down the polished oilcloth. 'Well – I don't know!' said Sister B. 'What ever are you doing that for?'

There's no accounting for these boys – tough and hard as they are – they have spirits, and are as light-hearted as children. One man was a 'quack doctor' the other evening. 'I can cure swellings in half an hour,' he shouted – looking around for a patient – my junior nurse held up a septic thumb to him I'd just wrapped up in a fomentation. 'Step up laddy, glad to see you,' he shot at her for all the world like a 'quack' on the Blackpool sands.

'You'd be very good looking, if it hadn't been for your face!' remarked a man looking down on a bed patient – he talked hard at him – close to his face.

'Don't splash!' answered the other, and went on listening to what he had to say, he was joking of course all the time – the lad in bed smiled.

'The Sergeant Major's fell off his horse!' is a favourite saying just now – and always brings the same reply from some other lad – 'Never mind the Sergeant Major – ride on! Trot!!'

They have fits for cheering – at times, they imitate 'going over the top', noise enough to raise the roof. Or on catching sight of me entering the ward – they'll say, 'Here's our nurse – let us greet her!' and the ward cheers! – Luckily we have 'B' Ward between 'A' Ward and Matron's room, I don't like shutting them up too much, even when they are noisy. It does them good I'm sure – to let off steam – and they appreciate a bit of 'easy going'.

'There goes a nurse who always has a smile for you!' said Hopley (my Sherwood Forester) the other evening.

'See her?' said another lad – 'Best little lass in hospital – best o' the lot!'.

I was writing in the ward one day – and a Tommy watched me from over the way. Presently he said, 'Put heaps o' love in, and tell him I'm asking after him!'

Poor old Coxon came to see the last of Moor Park a few weeks ago – he'd been at Blackpool since leaving us and his leg had healed (how long it will keep so, I should be afraid to say!) – he was on his way to Burton-on-Trent, his home – on furlough for 10 days.

'It'll be "over the top" for me now,' he said.

'Your bed in the corner – it's still there,' I said, pointing to it.

'Yes,' he said looking at it lovingly. 'My little bed, bless it!'

Coxon writes me long letters, he has quite an affection for his nurse. I hear three of our old boys have got commissions – well done! Watson (DLI), 'D' Ward, Usherwood (Essex Regt), 'A' Ward and Gemmell (HLI) of 'D' Ward.

I had a Dr's day, all to myself – last week. Sister B with others had gone up to the barracks to see Gen Sir Pitcairn Campbell give medals to the men. Dr Wilkins was very pleased with the way the men's wounds had done – I was glad, as I'd dressed those wounds myself for a month! He made some cuts in a septic thumb a nurse had and let me freeze it with ethyl-chloride, the spray is so fine and has to be held so far from the wound that it requires a very steady hand to aim at the right spot! Anyhow, we managed our job satisfactorily. I've done many jobs for Dr W now – even given anaesthetic – an out of the way proceeding for a 'VAD'.

When Sister B and the rest returned from the distribution of medals, they were full of excitement – for they'd been inspected with the men – and were lined up in the barrack square just behind some colonial troops and the General came and spoke to them.

I've had some interesting operations to help with – amongst them, I saw an eye removed (peppered with shrapnel dust) – Dr Sykes, eye specialist let me come right up to him – while he did it.

'Now this is one of the nastiest operations to watch!' he said as he worked away. 'Now you cut this and that – and now all is done, and there! You have the eyeball out of its socket!' and with a wee movement of an instrument out shot an ugly eye – round as a billiard ball onto the boy's forehead. He picked it up and explained it all and pulled the eye to bits for me, and picked out the tiny grains of shrapnel – a queer feeling to hold an eye in your fingers – it was one of the most interesting and cleanest operations I've ever seen. He really worked beautifully. I saw a bone-scraping one, and a cutting through and splicing a tendon (back of heel) to lengthen it – these lasted about an hour each.

* * * * *

Our last convoy of 210 men has been a business – we left the wards at 4 a.m. Virmy Ridge men, and men from Mochy and Arras – all wounded a week or so before we got them, and a most interesting lot – full of stories, of the big cavalry charge and of the tanks.

My men now (May 30th) are:

Ernst – Royal Canadians
Sgt Teagle – 2nd Leinsters
Baily – Warwickshire Regt
Bowden – RFA
Bishop – KR Rifles
Cowan – Royal Scots
Walsh
Jones – Canadian
Frost – Norfolk Regt
Wolfe
Griffiths – Machine Gun C
Woodrow – Royal Fusiliers
Hopley – Sherwood Foresters

Smith – Machine Gunner
Sgt McGlasham – 11th Hussars
Wright – Canadian
Swain – Cheshire Regt
Billaby – RFA
Lowther – RFA
Caterall – Machine Gun C
Firth – West Yorks Regt
Mansel – York & Lanc Regt
Cutche – R Sussex Regt
Hall – Hampshires
Youll – 1st Gordons

They are a nice cheery crowd. I'm senior in the ward, with two nurses under me. 'Now Sgt May,' they say for fun at me – 'What do you wish, give your orders, you're in command! Nurse, you love all your lads in y'r ward, don't you – we're all your lads!' 'She's our nurse!' they take up, one against the other. 'She's my nurse,' another will say. Up comes another – 'I tell you she's mine – she ain't yours!'

I laugh, and escape from the squabbling bunch by saying – for fun – 'Been a nice day, hasn't it Sergeant!' to someone who's not in this heated discussion and walk over to his bed – he quite 'springs' to the situation and the rest disperse in a (pretend) 'huff' with 'That's done it!'

We had high kippers for breakfast many a time lately! – either that, or they are salty. I used to be keen on a kipper! After trying to tackle one chap which proved too high for me one morning – I went into 'A' Ward – to hear shouting at me, 'Four to one Nurse de Trafford didn't enjoy her breakfast! Those herrings, Nurse, they were full of talk and they'd as many bones as I've got hairs on my head – phew! We had to shut the door to keep 'em out!'

'Yes,' said another lad, 'you know they got tired of the sea and surrendered! They'd have been better cooked in that (ether, that was being used in the dressings), it's like lemon peel that's been chained up for a long time.'

'Oh, them kippers, they've currants in their eyes. I refuse to pick 'em!'

*   *   *   *   *

Since writing these last pages, we've had another convoy of 66 stretcher cases – we turned a lot of our boys into the tents and took in 13 of these new ones. Terribly wounded – some. Usher, has a good quarter of his back blown away – an ugly wound – deep and hanging open wide – one's afraid to move him – he's dressed three times a day. Another has a leg, side, two wounds in arm and a hand the size of two with the thumb shattered off. Another has 14 pieces of shrapnel not yet removed, been X-rayed and pieces are marked with blue chalk on skin – shoulders, thigh and back – 'A nice job for theatre!' I said to Woodfin the other day when she was passing – as I pointed to him and he really looked like a blue spotted leopard.

A boy we have named 'Wolfe' (in 'A') is wounded in head, arm, side and has a big deep hole in his leg – poor chaps they are fairly smashed about! A fellow called Woodrow has to squirt his nose for deafness – 'Now then have you done your nose!' I asked.

'Yes,' replied a man from the opposite side of the ward – 'I saw him submerged this morning – nothing but a periscope sticking up!' Always ready with some quaint answer, funny boys.

'Wanting the owner of No. 8 bed,' I said to a lad. 'Are you 8?'

'No,' he said, 'I'm 30, me boot's 8s,' and his eyes gave a merry twinkle.

To hear the boys chattering always amuses me so, in the ward – I many a time laugh out loud. A fellow looked down at his slit-up sleeve that tied with 'umpteen' tapes round an arm splint. 'Say rats got at me last night – say I caught it on bed posts,' he remarked, dryly.

A man with a swollen face sat up in bed comically, and his next door neighbour remarked, 'Oh, 'e fell out of an aeroplane and caught his face on a steeple!'

I began taking the bandages off a foot. 'Oo-o-o-o! Dead Germans! – Poo! o-o-o the odour!' said some chatterbox of a boy – ''is toes'll come off wi' the dressing – o-o-o-o-o it's humming!' all the time holding his nose.

'Three new thermometers,' I said one day. 'Now a shilling fine for anyone who breaks one!'

A Scottie gazed thoughtfully looking at them in the glass of carbolic. 'A bob. Yes – that's three Bobs – Lord Roberts and 'is son, an' Bobbie Burrrrns!'

'You've got a boil?' I said one day. 'Sister B will squeeze it for you' (she's a great hand at this game).

'She's done it.'

'Oh, did she squeeze it?' I said, laughing.

'Yes, did she? She nearly lifted off her feet, she squeezed so hard.' There's no pity of no letting off for a Tommy with a boil once Sister B finds it – and he sits and tries to look pleasant while she delights in her 'squeezing' operation.

'Oh look, it's coming grand,' she'll say to me sometimes – while she amuses herself at Tommy's expense! 'Poo! That doesn't hurt!' she'll say, as he winces and she sets on him again with a will.

I saw a Tommy look down at another chap, who was tied to his bed. 'You're lazy,' he uttered at last – 'If you could do without breathing you wouldn't breathe at all.'

'I'll run you round the park for 2d!' said a fellow as he limped beside a man with a still bigger limp. 'I hope the German who hit me will have a head as big as an observation balloon!'

Someone asked a boy with a bandaged-up jaw what was the

'Black Watch' wears in his 'Balmoral' cap –saying, 'Would you like to have my buckle?' I hesitated, knowing it was as dear to him as his badge – as he'd worn it through his fighting out there in Salonica. 'Yes, I value it more than my badge,' he said – 'and can't I give it to whom I like?' I've had many little things given to me in this way, and one can't help feeling touched, and they find their way further into your heart than ever they've been before, these boys!

I heard from Payne a few days ago (I left for a fortnight's holiday before he went from the hospital). 'Wasn't it a wretched parting?' he said. 'It was very funny without you or Mon and I was in a bad temper in consequence – hoped you'd have come to say goodbye to Sister Kirkham and I might have had another glimpse of you – but no, you never came and my temper didn't improve! I didn't want to leave – especially to leave you!' Think he was nearly as devoted as Coxon.

Other 'H' Ward boys are: Whiting (shot through jaw and also through hand), Hutton, Green (a Canadian), Tuke (Yorkshire Yeomanry), Sgt Maj Smith, 'Jock' (Morrison), McArniny, Chapman (Ox and Bucks Regt), Boyle, Soloman (a S African), Mould, Sgt Wallis, Cruckshanks, Sgt Aires, Bloor, Batt, Williamson, Agnew (a Seaforth), Stanton, Gray, Sgt Gibbons (RFA), Taylor, Wilson, Tait, Barclay, Ramsey, Quay, McKenzie, Chivers, Carr, Dobson-Melville and Geldard – poor chap – one of our worse cases – left leg amputated below the knee, and right big toe off at joint – his head is badly bruised and discharging owing to sandbags having fallen on him – he's in a weary plight.

These Scots boys I love to hear them talk. We were to have had an inspection the other day. Spent all morning cleaning up – and none of us were allowed off in the afternoon, the men were all kept in too – such a fine day too – poor beggars – it was hard lines – and the General never came in the end. I saw one lad take some hot milk to a 'poorly man' – and as he stood by his bed holding the tray he said – 'Generals arrange an advance – and turn you out of a cushy trench. Go on, take your milk, it puts years on to me to watch you.' And a thin arm slowly wandered out from beneath the sheets and took the mug.

'Perhaps the morning rain damped him – this General! I suggested.

'No, he don't want damping, it's dumping he wants,' was a Tommy's remark.

They grumbled like anything about being kept in and no wonder. 'The Generrrrals ears will be rrrrringing,' said Mac, 'wi' so much being said about him.' 'I'll leave 'im a note on my bed,' said another, 'to say I'm awa'!' 'General humbug,' added another.

Over went a vase, on a locker top – the water streaming – 'Go for a mop! Quick!' we said – 'Let us gather up the river,' said a cheerful Scottie, as he set to work, glad of the job. Matron gave them an extension till 6 o'clock next day – she was annoyed at the General not coming – I managed to iron out my Pierrot trousers however in the ward kitchen!

We had a concert that same evening – for the men. 6 p.m. till 8 p.m. – it went very well and we returned to 'H' Ward – in our Pierrot garb and finished our work there – 'suppers', 'pills and medicines' and putting men to bed who'd been brought down on stretchers to see our concert.

'Nurse, you make a dandy boy!' said a Canadian to me.

'I wish you'd always wear those clothes in the ward!' said another.

'He's a nice chap,' said Sgt Aires – to Wallis, 'Nurse, he and I met a married woman and a single one – Wallis palmed off the married one on me, and "allied" away with the single one.' I love the word 'ally' being used in this way.

We've a Scotch laddie, 'Quay' – he's the life of the Ward – we get him to sing to us in the evening and very well he sings too – ragtimes and a few love songs too and his amusing face and Scots accent and soft tenor voice I can hear now.

'Now Quay, mind you are in for roll call.'

'Och, sure', he'd reply.

'Here now I'll give you my gold watch,' said Sister Jock, 'and don't be late – it worries me when my men are absent at roll call!'

'Och – I wouldn't worrrry you for a' the worrrrld – I'll take yer watch, Sister, and wear it next me hearrrrt.' Sister winked at me – she loved this lad – who could help it – and still, who, if any was absent from 'roll'? Why it was sure to be Quay. Woodfin would call – Pte McKenzie? Sister. Pte McAnany? Sister. L.ple Ramsey? Sister, and so on, all would answer 'Sister' till she called 'Pte. Quay?' Again 'Pte Quay?' Not a sound – 'All in, except Quay' – Woodfin would say – turning smartly to carry on roll calling in other wards. Some time after, that gentleman would appear.

'Quay, you are late! The roll's been called.' From Sister Jock 'Where have you been?'

'Out, as usual,' was his straight reply, and his face would twinkle and pucker up in a most irresistible way – 'Been talking to a lass at the railings – she's ma dearrrest adorrrable – she's only a wee handful, but she's worth her weight in gold – I fell in wi' her.'

'You had my watch – there's no excuse – off you go to the office to Sister Woodfin,' said Sister Jock. Matron tackled him – 'You were out?' and looking her straight in the face he said, 'Rrrrrright enough I was!' One evening looking at Jock's gold watch he said, 'Thank you Sister – oh, a'll be back by seven – does yer watch often ga astray?' (Longing for an excuse to be late again and to have a word with his 'dearest adorable') 'Och! this love-making, will drive me off the face o' the earth!' he said.

The other night four men were out, about 20 minutes after 'roll call' – down they were sent to Woodfin – it's always a job for that good-hearted lass to be severe and Sister Jock made signs to them to keep serious. Woodfin met the procession in the passage and rated them fine! Next morning they and the others from other wards (also absent at 'roll') were brought up before Matron – she gave them 'labour' for two hours a morning for about a week – very hot weather too – and our four were put on the job of moving a rough pile of soil and brickbats from outside the new hostel – right opposite our 'H' Ward windows – and then digging a border all the way under the hostel windows. They came draggling in to dinner – melting with heat – 'And all this for kissing a girl,' mumbled one. One has to be strict with them, or they'd be out all hours.

* * * * *

October

Great excitement, Matron has received 'The Royal Red Cross' for her services – a decoration which is given by the King. We all trooped in to her office and congratulated her. She was very beaming.

'Well of course I'm very pleased and proud – but I consider it reflects credit on all my nurses, and staff of the hospital – I should be nowhere without you.' Pretty decent of the old lady.

'Jock' and Woodfin are both mentioned for their services – in the list of 'Women's work for the wounded.' We've had two convoys – in ten days. One of 76 and one of 28, all from France. We've had our hands full and were three weeks without 'half days off'. I've enjoyed the work though, and they are a nice lot of lads – and appreciate everything, so it's a pleasure to work for them and help them. One thing is everyone is bright and cheery – men, sisters and nurses and that means so much and it's well worth the trouble and tiredness and weary legs etc. to be amongst them. I heard it said the other day that the only really bright and cheerful places were our hospitals – things are sad, lonesome and dreary in England these days – and with all the Tommies' light-heartedness and bright little sayings, and our way of talking and amusing them as they fire away their little remarks and funny dry speeches, all go to make the time pass happily and pleasantly for us, and we take no end of interest in the boys. Our worst case in 'H' (in fact the worst the hospital's ever had), came in the '28 convoy' – he's just mutilated, blown to bits! – the doctors say they ought never to have sent him over. What the journey must have been! He has right toe amputated, left leg blown off nearly up to the thigh, right hip torn open and a huge hole burrowed into it by shrapnel – two deep holes between his shoulder blades – two scars on his forehead, and his thumb damaged. It takes us three quarters of an hour to do his dressings, and a sister and two nurses at work all the time – Reoch, ('Jock' as we call him) is a 'Black Watch' – and so Scotch! It took a long time to get used to his lingo.

94

We have 25 Australians with us – such fine good-looking fellows too – twelve have gone to 'F' Ward – I believe I am to have 'F' soon, when I start night duty. The 'H' boys are very distressed at my leaving them. 'Wish you weren't going,' said Ellis (a 1st Norfolk). 'Can we do anything to stop it? I'll go and ask Matron to stop it, and not to change you!'

* * * * *

Well here I am – night duty and acting as staff nurse. The wards of the hospital are divided. 'A', 'B', 'C' and 'D' at one end and 'E', 'F', 'G', 'H', at the other. Two Sisters are on duty – one each end and each has two staff nurses who relieve each other. Staff Nurse Williams and I relieve each other and we are on the 'E', 'F', 'G', 'H' side of the hospital, Nurses Wilkins and Spencer are acting Staff nurses on the other end (i.e. 'A', 'B', 'C', 'D'). Williams and I take it turn and turn about as to our times 'on' and 'off duty'. One night I have 10.30 p.m. to 1 a.m. off, and she has 1 to 5, the next night we reverse things, she having 10 to 1 and I 1 to 5. At 5.30, when hard work begins, I am in 'F' Ward and 'G' only – beds, washings, medicines and temperatures and I write my own report – during this time I am sent a junior nurse to help with the beds or whatever I order her to do.

'F' is a 29 bed ward, and 'G' a 6 – so my work is set out! During the night I have 'H', 32 beds, 'G' 6, 'F' 29 and 'E' 30, about 96 men to attend to! 'F' Ward requires most attention – trench fever men, and one with mental delusions keeps me on the hop – not knowing what he'll do next, this fellow (Reynolds), an Australian – can't sleep, brain too active – says he wants to 'get out and gallop round the hospital' (to use his own words) - tells me he over-taxed his brain while studying at University – his one idea is getting out of doors – and I found him in the cold passage rattling at a side door, saying if only he could get out nobody would see him again. Sometimes he will be sitting at the table in the centre of the ward – at 1 or 2 a.m., huddled in a dressing gown – writing pages and pages with just a glimmer of light – 'I must do something, or go mad,' he'll say to me – I eventually get him to return to bed and get him his sedative mixture. (That bottle! What should we do without it!)

95

Sister and I had such a hunt one evening and she discovered him having taken refuge in the quiet spot – old 'E' Ward lavatory, behind the door writing his usual lengthy letters on the table used for arranging flowers on. He's a very nice boy, and it's a pity to see him nervy and restless like this – 'It's my brain,' he'll tell me sometimes.

There's a poor chap in 'H side ward' desperately ill with cancer – I've never seen anyone look so ill or so terribly thin – perfectly ghastly – and when he is asleep – propped up with a dozen pillows, he looks like a dead man, hollow temples – ashen grey face and bones standing out in his cheeks and head like a skull – he's so sick and bad and wants constant attention – He generally has a special nurse but as often as not I relieve – many hours I've spent watching him, it's awful seeing him getting worse and worse every day and one can do nothing for him. It seems he had a terrible drop down a pit or disused quarry (70 feet fall) and this shook and bruised him internally and started the cancer. Sometimes when he wakes he is only half conscious and stretches his arms and hands out – it would give anyone (not accustomed to seeing him) a shock if they went in to his ward and saw him lying there – it will be a merciful release when he dies – poor Hayes!

'Nurse,' said an 'F' boy one night – 'they say you are missed very much in "H".'
  'Oh,' I replied, 'Why?'
  'Soldiers told me so in the town,' he said.
  'Oh,' I laughed, 'Soldiers talk!'
  'Here,' I said once to an 'H' boy, 'Will you roll me a bandage for "F"?'
  'Yes, nurse, of course, wouldn't we do anything for you,' came the quick reply.
  'Yes, I think I can get round any of you – can't I?' I said laughing, as I chucked him the heap of unrolled bandage.
  'Yes, I think we can get round you too,' he said with a merry twinkle in his eye.
  I'd been into 'H' before going off duty the other morning – Ellis

96

opened the ward door and stood while I passed out – 'Exit! Heroine!' he said – 'You don't belong to 'F' Ward, we won't have it!'

'Oh dear, no,' I laughed – 'I'm only let out on hire!' Last Christmas Day I started night duty and Matron said it wouldn't be right to let us go on again – so got me on early to let me have Christmas free – and we shall only just manage to get in our month before then. We come off December 22nd.

*　　*　　*　　*　　*

Matron has got her Royal Red Cross – she went up to London – to Buckingham Palace and the King pinned it on – he and the Queen spoke to her – and Queen Alexandra too, who asked her about the hospital, its size, etc. and congratulated her when she heard we now have over 260 beds – and she asked her to take back her well wishes to her 'Sister' and nursing staff. Poor old Matron – she was bombed the very night she arrived and spent the night in a cellar somewhere – received her RRC at 10 a.m., the following morning, and got back here at 11 p.m.

Matron's eldest son (in the REs) was killed a week or so ago – it's been a great blow to the old lady – he was a fine looking boy – we put him up in one of the small wards when he got leave from the front a few months ago.

Now to return to 'F' Wards' sayings and doings – some of the boys' funny little sayings – so quaint and said on the spur of the moment and just to the point! The old hour 5.30 a.m. comes round – that I described when on night duty last year. I switch on the electric lights ('F' is very up to date, and 'H' also – and sports electric lights!).

I tug at the bedclothes of one lad – his next door neighbour looks out with one eye over the top of his blankets – 'He'll get up in time, Nurse, 'is heart's good enough, but 'is mind won't let 'im!'

Others are so wrapped up in sheet and blankets and curled round into circles that one can scarcely unwind them – and you have to excavate before you get down deep enough to discover the man!

'Come on!' I keep saying – 'Get up, there's a good chap, and give us a hand – I've only got one nurse to help me with all these beds – and there's the breakfast to fetch!'

One by one they (those who can) roll out of bed – yawning and rubbing their eyes. 'Alright, nurse, I'm coming,' and once they are up begins that everlasting little leg play and chaff – that they carry on with all the day long! – Wonderful chaps.

They'll paddle out for a wash and shave – in pyjamas – top coats, dressing gowns – and every conceivable garb – some will return with their chins cut and bleeding – 'Nurse, I've cut myself!'

'There,' I say – as I pick a fluffy piece of wool off the swab I'm wiping the carbolic off the ends of the thermometers with. 'Stick that on, it'll stop the bleeding!'

'Eh, 'e's been trying to cut 'is throat at the back,' some fellow will remark – 'And now 'e's got wool growing' (seeing my bit of fluffy wool sticking on to the cut).

Another boy will come into the ward with his chin lathered – he'll look across to where I'm standing, 'Father Christmas half frosted!' he'll say with a laugh. Shouts from Scott (an Australian who is now sitting up in bed), he holds a hot water bottle high up over his head. 'An addition to the family!'

Another 'F' Ward boy asks for his morning 'Carsbad salts'.

'Very well,' I say as I leave my job I'm busy at – to fetch him his salts – another man will remark – 'You might think 'e wants to turn his self in to corned beef – 'e wants so much salts!'

They set to with the breakfast about 6.30 a.m., and all is quieter then as they stuff it down.

'Nurse, what do those two blokes want, they're on milk diet.'

'Oh, yes, alright, you get your breakfast, boy, I'll see to them,' I say – and off I go to forage for milk or the like stuff!

'Once we were shelled while having our breakfast,' said a Royal Scot – and it gave us "tinko"!' (whatever 'tinko' was – I'm sure it was a hot time for someone!).

'A German had four shots at me and hasn't killed me yet,' said one boy.

'Oh,' said another – 'Fritz had to set a cathedral a'fire before 'e could see me, to shoot at me!'

98

Some lad would start a song, 'Oh some singer,' I'd say as I shook down a thermometer with vigour!

'No, you can't sing the noo,' replied Seaforth Highlander.

'Yes, you can, sing again!' I said.

'No, birrrrrds have to wait till daylight,' he answered – (there's precious little light anyway at 6.30 in December!).

'I heard Matron's cock crowing at 3 a.m., and I wasn't sure if it was you, "Jock", or the cock!' I said to tease him. You must keep on cracking little jokes with them and you get into the way of it so, somehow.

There's a funny chap, Jackson, in 'F'. He 'clucks' in his sleep. I often stand while passing down the ward during the night and laugh out loud – at him. 'My word you were clucking last night,' I remark, next morning, as I work away at the bedmaking.

'Yes, nurse,' some boy will answer, 'I saw you come in and stand listening to him – he often does that – we'll get him a sitting of eggs and put 'em in his bed, he may fancy he's a hen!'

Clucking or no clucking, I'm only too glad when they'll sleep, and he can. 'What's the matter – can't you sleep?' I sometimes say to a moaning man – 'I do feel all shaken about somehow, nurse!' or 'I'm too tired to sleep and oh me legs do ache,' from a trench fever man – which means I have to start rubbing them with oil or 'methsal' – and swathe them up in wool and bandages – and give them aspirins or quinine and hot drinks and raise their feet on pillows – in half an hour's time I creep back and it's such a relief to find them asleep – trench fever men have awful pains in their limbs. Gaskell and Warwick are about the worst I have to deal with, with this complaint and if one isn't bad the other is!

There's been a convoy while I've been on 'nights' – and I got six fresh cases in 'G' Ward and four in 'F' – mostly nephritis and trench fever – and one fractured ribs – a funny little Russian is amongst these new men – he stands 4ft 2 ins – hideously ugly – with huge standing-out ears – 'Ears like an imp in "John Bull" paper,' as a man remarked to me one day – he speaks very broken English and can't write much in our writing – I had to address two letters for him the first morning, his own writing (Russian) is more like Japanese – he spent some years in Manchester before he 'joined up' – has picked up Lancashire without knowing it. How are you? 'Middlin',' he'd answer.

These convoys – they are so frequent now they cease to excite us now, we were literally disappointed once if told the day staff would not be required to help the night – as the convoy was small that was coming. Still, there's always a certain amount of interest about it. 'What cases have you got?' 'Which ward has the least cases?' 'How many new ones have you got?' – 'Any stretcher cases?' 'Any gassed men?' – 'Any amputations?' And the worse the wounds, the better pleased we are!

'When the troops come home it's a rough night, isn't it?' said one of our old boys.

'See the fallen heroes come, the stragglers return!' sang out another.

I heard a Tommy say one day, looking at a bundle of filthy trench clothes just taken off a new arrival from France – 'If you addressed that lot it might walk up to the stores by itself!' Rather good I thought.

'Have some tea?' I said to a new Tommy. 'No thanks,' he smiled, 'Tea would be shouting hurra on the top of the coffee!' (he'd been liberally supplied at the station buffet with coffee, before being conveyed up to hospital).

I love seeing our old boys helping a new helpless chap into his nice clean clothes – though they don't always fit first try on! A small boy will invariably get a big shirt, the sleeves of which hang over his wrist, 'Never mind!' says his willing helper – 'It was made for your growth!' In the meantime I am struggling with socks that are so muddy and shrunk that they will hardly leave his feet. Oh the efforts and the struggles of a convoy night! They seem to feed the Tommies well in France – good white bread, they say, and not this war bread we are now getting – 'I saw so many chickens in one hospital I was at in France,' said one man to me – 'that I felt I couldn't look a fowl in the face again!'

They keep talking about the huge rats they have in the trenches – they all tell you the same story – how tame they are and how big!

'When lying half asleep, you'll feel 'em on yer coat sleeve –

and then you feel their old bushy whiskers up against yer face,' a 1st Norfolk (Sgt Clarke) told me the other day.

That poor chap Hayes died a few night ago, I'm glad it's over for him. I was with him practically up to his death – I left him at 2 a.m. – quite unconscious, pulse weak and breathing just in gasps – at 2.40 he died. He was a plucky fellow and never complained, said one day to one of our 'H' men – 'I wonder if I shall be alive to see the end of the war, sometimes I don't know if I'm alive or dead!' – (and really we didn't know if he was dead or not – he looked so awful and there was such a long pause between his breathing).

I went to have my rest (2 a.m. to 5) a few nights ago. I curled up on the sofa in our little sitting room and lit the gas fire and slept on blissfully till 4 a.m. – when I heard creakings of some door being opened – thinking they were calling me for some reason an hour earlier I lifted my head from the blankets and looked about me. It was not what I thought – it was Woodfin's door that was opening – out came a more than miserable creature in pyjamas rubbing her head and her eyes full of sleep – and a truly wretched voice said – 'Traffy! There are mice in my bed and they've been running over my hair! Come and look,' so I toddled in after her and examined the bed and pillows – and certainly found plenty of evidence that a mouse had been running round!

'Traffy, what shall I do – I no likey!' went on poor Woodfin – so I said, 'Tuck yourself up on my sofa and I'll get into the armchair!' – which we did – the mouse was a stranger evidently and it kept trying to get out of her room – jumping up against the door and sliding down again.

Next day we had a trap set and had no luck – that evening I was in the room – Woodfin went to draw the curtain.

'Traffy, I believe it's here!' she said, and I got a flashlight and found Mr Mouse in a ledge above the window – oh how we laughed and what a chase we had! Sister Lanter assisted – and in the end she and I lay on our tummies under the bed and got the mouse cornered under a rucked piece of oil cloth – Sister L got her hand underneath while I held the other side down and caught the offender in her hand alive – and took him into her Ward ('E') – where the boys made short work with him.

They had great games with the night staff – hung it up by the tail to the medicine cupboard and then asked a nurse passing through the ward to fetch a pill or some medicine for them. Then screams from the 'mouse scared creature' and shouts of laughter of course from the men. They tried it on with me – 'Nurse, I want a No. 9.'

'Do you?' I said, 'I suppose you want me to scream at the mouse. I'm not frightened of it – in fact I helped catch it!' So it fell somewhat flat, for them!

Well I've done with 'F' Ward and night duty once more, and have got back into 'H'. I went home for Christmas, for four days. An 'H' man saw me the day I left – 'So you aren't going to spend Christmas with us – and after we've been breaking our necks to get you back again!'

Anyhow Christmas Day was on Tuesday, and on Wednesday morning (or rather midday) I was back amongst them again. The hospital was extremely well decorated this year and beat last year I think. The night I returned there was a bran pie for the men and nurses, and a concert, whist drive, dance or something each night for quite a fortnight – the Christmas tree was on Christmas Day, this I missed, but got my present from Matron off it.

One night we really had great fun – a fancy dress dance – the dresses were remarkably good – some were made-up ones, whilst some had their own good dresses which they were allowed to wear. We were classed in two lots – those who wore make-up's and those who wore real fancy dresses – and two prizes (a lady's and man's) given in each class. I wore my Spanish dress, and let my hair down, Woodfin got a first prize as a rajah, perfectly excellent she was, white turban of butter muslin – jolly well put on too, white Dr's slip – more muslin, which I draped for her over her shoulders to hang like a coat – and a great big oriental sash, which I got from home, tied round her waist – she looked fine – quite a handsome rajah! Little black moustache and browned skin – we had many a dance that night – our steps suit each other – 'I can dance better with Traffy than anyone,' I head her telling someone.

102

We had an inspection by General Sir Pitcairn-Campbell the other day – jolly old boy, he is always so nice to the boys – a little conversation and a pat on the shoulder for each – he's a huge man and looks most imposing – followed by five staff officers. 'Well nurses!' he said to us three, standing by the ward door – 'I hope you're comfortable here – Matron fed you well and all that?' He wanted to know if we lived in hospital and finding Anderton and I did, he asked various questions as to our welfare – in front of Matron! and we caught an amused twinkle in the eyes of his 'staff'! He's the General commanding the 'Western Command,' headquarters Chester – Maj. Farquarson was one of his staff. I wish all our inspections were by him – so often we polish and clean and keep the men in – and then only get a few grunty words – from some old 'dug out' General or Colonel.

We've lost Sgt Clarke (1st Norfolks) – he was quite a character in the hospital – knew everyone and every scrap of hospital news. He's seen three years and four months' service at the front – and has the DCM, Mons Medal and Military Medal. Entered the Regt at 15 (in the drums) – been to India, S Africa and was most interesting in his stories and description of things. I've often sat listening with three or four 'joined for the war' Tommies, who listened with interest to his stories of India – their sports, and big game shooting, and all the life of a 'peace time' Tommy – from that he'll turn to the treat from Mons – most vivid description of all the awful horrors and German atrocities he saw with his own eyes. He was a most good natured man under the sun – do anything for anybody – 'Anything lost? – Oh ask the Sergeant.'

We shall miss him. He'd take the keenest interest in every little thing – and quite settled himself down to the life!

'You're happy here aren't you?' I'd say laughing at his fat beaming face.

'That I am, it's home from home!' I never saw a chap eat (and enjoy it so), as that fellow, if you'd a scrap of food over from some concoction you were making for a bad case – you'd only to say, 'Here you are Sergeant!' and he'd whip it up and toss it into his mouth – always first down to the dining hall. 'Come on lads!' he'd shout at the ward door, 'Bell's gone,' and he'd go at a gallop, sideways like a crab – my, he must have put on weight during the time he spent with us! He made a polite speech to me, and quite to the point one day, 'My belly's like a pawn shop, it'll take anything!' We told him Gen. Sir P-Campbell would notice him and 'mark him out' – and funnily enough – he was walking up the ward – talking to this man and that – and when he went up to Sgt Clarke – he said looking round at his staff officers – 'Look at this chap! Fit for a show – doesn't he look well?' and he hooked him by the button and drew him up to him – much to the amusement of us all.

The other night the sergeant sat talking to Stumble and me – India again – he made us both roar with laughter! They keep mynah birds in their barrack rooms he said, they got very tame and hopped about from bed to bed eating up the bugs and livestock – also parrots – crowds of them. 'We had 40 parrots in a hut of 50 men – also a few mynah birds!' he said. 'Coming home the Capt offered a prize for the nearest guess as to the number of parrots on board – 570 men on the ship – and there were 1,300 parrots – 400 only got to England alive. You can buy a parrot for 2d out there – or you can buy 'em in exchange for an old khaki coat what's worn out,' he added. 'It's 12 years since I came home and I have one of the two parrots I brought – I thought it would "roll up" on the way being the most delicate – but it was the one who lived – talks fine – call the cat it do and says, "Wake up mother, daylight's come. Set the fuse – and fire the gun." We keep 'im in a T, and it catches all the trouble.' (I love the expression – polly's seed and mess being called 'trouble').

This sergeant said a great game was catching big black crows that used to come in through the doors and windows to steal butter and eatables (in India) and tying long pieces of wood like stilts to their feet – then letting them go and watching them hobble off down the polished floor – click-clacking – if they flew off and got outside in the trees, crowds of other birds and parrots too would fly round and peck the wretched 'bird on stilts' to death. A cruel performance, but the idea of a crow on stilts so tickled my fancy, it made me laugh and laugh when he told me and the quaint way he has of clipping his words adds to the funniness of it. I thought too, the idea of keeping mynah birds was a brainy notion! As he said,

'You don't know what company there is – some blankets are as lousy as cuckoos!' That's enough about the sergeant – he'd talk for hours.

* * * * *

We've just had a new convoy – 146 – from France (Feb:1918). We've a nice lot of men – six Canadians – five Guardsmen and an assortment of every kind of Regt in 'H' Ward. There are quite a lot of the guards in the hospital – mostly gassed men – nice fellows.

Today I saw two big good-looking fellows sweeping my ward. 'Hullo,' I said as I passed. 'Swept by the Grenadiers!' – 'This job seems to be left to the Guards,' laughed one of them with a merry twinkle – there's a nice '2nd Scots', one of Rogen T's lot – and an 'Irish Guards' – who knew Noel Durant, Charlie Moor and young Clifford well.

We still have 'Jock' – the man with eight wounds – he's wonderfully well and is out on crutches – he'd a nasty tumble a few days ago – got his crutches down a grid somewhere in the town and fell on his stump, poor chap it's very raw yet, it gave him 'gyp' as the boys say and started it bleeding.

Poor 'Jock', he was very excited the other day – his brother called to see him on his way back to the Front – I found him talking to him with all his kit – water bottle, strappings, tin hat, rifle, etc. in a heap on the floor – they talked brightly enough together, presently the brother got up quite silently – went to the heap of kit – two Tommies helped him on with everything – he looked like an over-weighted Christmas tree – he looked round and nodded to the lads – and us – and left the ward by the window-door. It was snowing hard and looked so dreary compared with the bright cheery ward, he disappeared into the darkness, one of our boys going to the gate with him – he'd gone, back to fight, and Jock sat quite still, head lowered and tears rolling out of his eyes – even this hardy old 'Black Watch' was moved – and one felt heartache too, good luck to him poor fellow.

'Jock' is such an old Scottie! I love to hear him talk – when a doctor comes and looks at him he retires under the sheets.

105

'Ministers and doctors I no delicht in at all, when they call at home – I go oot o' the room' – he tells me when I tease him after the doctor's gone – Dr Healy laughed at him the other day. Jock held his head low – for all the world like a shy child – 'Come along, Jock,' he said cheerily – lifting up his chin and raising his head – 'Scotland forever!'

'Nursie, can you no pull it a wee bit tichter,' Jock will say to me sometimes as I bind up his stump – 'Ach! That's fine! Where's the prin? (pin).'

I started a 'Taffie' talking Welsh the other day – Jock listened chuckling to himself. 'I no understand thee mon, do ye talk like that in yer din hairn?' I always love hearing Jock's talk – most attractive! Here's a nice little saying – 'Nurse, what's me temper, an' how many coonts me pulse?' he said, holding on to his little stump (about a foot long that's all it is). 'Me leg's sair it was a' I could do to keep it from crumping last night! My sister used to greet cos she were no' a man – folk are softer wi' the lassies – but I was alright – they were gude to me – as I was a bairrrrrn!'

'When I was asking for me good looks,' said a little 'fighting 5th' opposite to Jock the other day – 'The door was shut in me face!' (such a description).

By the way this little chap Tait – left us today – 17 months he's spent with us here – quite an incurable I should think – he said to me when I said good night to him, 'Nurse it will be alright if I die in the night,' he did so dread leaving us the following morning. He went in our Red Cross ambulance to Whalley – with four other men – Sister Woodfin went with them – and sat on the box seat and got a blow – different sisters go each time – it's a nice drive and also they like seeing the big hospital (2,000 beds there). Woodfin said Tait nearly broke down as he shook hands with her when she left the boys there – his eyes were welling over as he said in a quiet little voice, 'Goodbye Sister!' She was the last glimpse of Moor Park – which had been 'home' for him for so long.

We had another little dance the other evening – men and nurses – they are quite fun – my '2nd Scots Guards' had three or four walzes with me – (Cowan) – a nice fellow – a gassed Grenadier said he'd tried to dance but got 'as giddy as a goat' – and found himself 'gasping like a cod fish – you know how a cod fish gasps?' he said merrily – good old Bailey – he's a great favourite and the life of 'H' Ward – he and Cowan are a bright pair – always got something funny to say – they're smart fellows these Guardsmen – Bailey had me drilling with a broomstick the other evening (à la Guards!). 'Slope – arms.' 'Order – arms!' 'Present!' and quite enjoyed getting me into shape.

Some of their little stories amuse me hugely and I only wish I could put them down here as they tell me them, but one misses their merry peels of laughter and their teasing and jibing at one another about the achievements of their own regiments – a man's regiment is always better than the other man's he's arguing with.

'The Black Watch was in action before the "Fighting Fifth" – me lad,' some Jock will let fly.

'Not them!' 'Hey!' (to another of his lot further down the ward) 'Weren't we first to fire a shot at Fritz!' and so on – heated discussions go on – which end by a knowing wink and a friendly clap on the back probably.

'Eh – Nurse!' will say some infantry man – 'have you heard the latest?' 'No, what?' I say and waving a sketch or mirror high over his head says in a deriding voice – 'The Guards have been in action,' (just to tease the Guards) – and just for fun I reply with a look at one of my Grenadiers – 'Guards in action – of course, you bet they were there!'

'Soldiers 1d each!' will sing out some lad – and a gassed voice of a Guardsmen will huskily shout – '6d soldiers us!' to which the other regiments pretend to turn up their noses and look with disdain at the big tall fellows – and a moment after one boy will remark in a lower voice to me 'Smart boys – pride and pick of the British Army!' and so they are.

Cowan (Scots Gds) told me about how they pulled up a row or two of potatoes at some French billet and stuck the stalks in the ridges (minus potatoes!). The old farmer's wife I suppose went to pull some up and they came up loose in the hand – angry was no word for it! 'Offic'ere, where is the offic'ere?' and she made a bee-line for Capt – and demanded 50 francs – she made such a to-do he gave it to her willingly, saying, 'It was cheap at the price, to get rid

107

of her,' – but he thoroughly enjoyed a joke and laughed like anything.

*　*　*　*　*

It is May now – and I've skipped a big lot that ought to be written – three convoys more – have been got in. 120 – 76 – and 111. The 120 came mostly from the retreat of St Quintin, with terrible stories to relate, lots of hospitals had to be evacuated – the Germans came pressing on and those who could, started to walk – or get on what Red Cross waggons they could, others had to crawl and drag shot legs after them. One man told me – they tried to get a scratch band together (not worthy of the name 'band') – to play them on – all nurses, although they protested, were sent off. Another poor chap in my ward said he had been struggling along for a couple of miles with a wounded leg, when a rough ammunition cart came up alongside of him – on top of it was seated a Captain in the 'Buffs'. He shouted for my man to be helped up to where he was, on the cart. The Captain had one leg completely shot away – he gave my boy brandy out of his flask and then he fainted.

'I suppose you think I'm a baby, sir, to faint,' he said.

'Not a bit of it lad – you're all a plucky lot of boys – every one of you,' answered the Captain, 'and something to be proud of.' This is just a little incident which shows their willingness to help others.

We've got two 'runners' in the ward – battalion runners – 'I took the message for re-enforcements but I never got back to the regiment again,' said one the other day to me, as we did a very hard job, this runner job – and yet every regiment must have them to run messages to Head Quarters.

'You do all this work without any pay, nurse?' said a Tommy to me one day. 'You ought to get paid, you mend up blokes instead of killing 'em.' (As if to show the difference between us – 'Nurse' and 'Tommy').

Tommy is very quick, and says things to the point at a moment's notice – Coward's van (provision merchant and grocer to the hospital) entered the gate and went past the ward windows. 'See,' called out a lad – 'I bet that chap was a conscientious objector!'

'What are you – oh RAMC? – that's robbers and murderers combined.' I heard this shouted, shouted from one to another. I laughed. 'That's a new version,' I said. 'We nurses say "Run away Matron's coming"!' This pleased them no end, and they laughed heartily.

Evidently one man's step-father was a mean sort of chap – as I overheard this – 'Second bloke me mother married, he'd kill a pig and give 'an ear to the poor.' Such a description. This seems a funny disconnected part of the book – but these odd fragments of talk amused me at the time, though they lose their funniness in having to write them down.

One Tommy (minus a leg) sat watching a battery of RFA pass the windows, 'Och, there go the mob, they're richt for a joy ride the day.' A pencil rolled from the next man's locker onto the floor – 'Pick it up Jock lad,' said its owner – 'Och-awa' wi' yer! You're a nuisance to the trrrrooops.' I try and copy their Scots and they laugh – 'Och I'll mak' a Scottie o' yer yet,' they say. 'Say "a wee pochleie",' that means a wee bittie.

What was the Hippodrome like I asked Jock – 'Putrrrrrid' he announced – 'if it had been much worse it would have been real bad!' A good advertisement for the Hippodrome, wasn't it? I always did like the Jocks and their quaint sayings and rolling r's.

'What regiment are you in? Oh the KRRs'.

'The K ha! ha!' added the clown of the ward, 'Tich'.

I am to do a month's night duty, I hear. Spencer is away for a week so I take duty in 'E' Ward from 5 to 8 a.m. and in the night I'm in 'H', 'F' and 'E' Wards – also have some special gas cases in the side wards. I am to sleep out this time – as more girls are in the cubes. Here I am on nights – the 'E' boys are a nice lot and I get on well with them. Sister Cooper is on at my end of the hospital – Sister Waterfield at the other. Spencer has returned and takes 'E' now (her own ward). I have 'H' and the side wards.

A new convoy has arrived – which makes us very busy indeed – 37 gassed cases amongst them, poor chaps, and they are bad! I have four of the worst in the side wards – and I am at it most of the night through, giving them drinks – sometimes only a half teaspoon at a time or else they choke – their chests are fearfully bad and eyes all bloodshot and made up with matter – some are burnt with mustard gas – eyelids and foreheads – which adds to their misery. Temperatures to take four-hourly, and a list made for each man, food given – how much and what quantity, so these four 'specials', and 'H' Ward with various wounds to dress and put fomentations on, and all the beds to make, with the help of one orderly and a junior nurse, keep one on the go. Sister Cooper is very willing to work and give a hand where it's heavy, but she has three wards and can't be everywhere! I am sleeping very well on days – so that's a great thing!

I had a terrible time with a lunatic – poor wretched chap – he'd most dirty ways – I can never describe what it was like looking after him. He just wallowed in filth and one night we had to change his bedclothes about five times, it nearly made one sick, and I can stand a good lot – not easily put off – he used to get mucked up from his bandaged leg splint to his fingertips – and also used to rake one foot against the bad leg and in doing this he loosened the bandage and dressing – most awful language he used! and pulled such grimaces! – poor unhappy fellow! We had a bank clerk doing orderly one evening and he and I had a really bad time with him. He came to me and (though highly amused) he said in a solemn voice – 'That chap is throwing wool and filth about the room.' 'Oh,' I laughed, 'be prepared for that, he's always in that state!' 'Oh,' he replied, 'as long as we know!' He got so rough we had to get a folded sheet under him, round his body and tie him to the bed, bringing the end of the sheet under the mattress and safety pinning it down on the other side of the bed. Neither the clerk or I will ever forget that chap!

We laughed a great deal – and the fact of our loony behaving was in those ways (disgusting though it was!) got too much for us, and we just had fits of giggling – couldn't help it! We'd get him changed and clean and then he'd say 'Nurse, you're alright with him now – and keep an eye on the joker and I'll be back again in no time.'

Off he'd go to get a bit of supper or something – and I was left to the loony and his grimaces – he'd a bad self-inflicted wound, poor beggar – which had to be dressed – he'd a trick of pulling up the

110

bedclothes tight over his face and tucking them under his head and he'd lie like a man in a coffin. He was always and forever asking for a chocolate. 'Nurse, have you got a chocolate.' One night he bothered us so, that we raided some man's locker in the 'tents' and found some – he plucked them out of our hands and stuffed them into his mouth and immediately inquired, 'Nurse, have you got a chocolate?' It was the same question – till one was sick and tired of having him. We couldn't manage him – he was taken off by ambulance to Winnick Asylum, a nice handful for someone to look after if he continued in his ways!

Moor, Connington, Reid and Penn were my four gassed men. Reid (a 'tank corps') was frightfully bad – so was Moor, still they are getting on capitally – in fact they've gone into their own wards now and Sister 'Jock' said to me the other night – 'Those men have got on so well we've taken them back and sent you a worse case out of 'B' Ward.'

Well all things end – and so has my month's night duty. I've had two nights at home and have come back to find I am Senior Nurse of 'D' Ward – with a junior who has been in the wards a fortnight – so again my work is cut out! I have 14 beds – and the men are a good, willing lot, and will do all they can to give me any help they can. 'Nurse we'd do anything for you!' one said to me the other day.

A convoy came a few nights ago (90 or so), a great many have been in the big bombing raid on Etaples – 1,500 casualties – and five hospitals hit – 300 killed and wounded at one hospital. It's rough luck when a man is lying wounded, to be blown out of bed and wounded, by falling bombs and roof and building materials tumbling onto him. They give frightful descriptions of the sights – legs and arms wrenched off, men tossed out of wards, trolleys, bottles, beds all flying about. Seventy poor sisters and nurses were killed, and were buried in one big funeral in the soldiers' cemetery. One man (Webb) I have in 'D', tells me he was carrying a man on his back from a bombed ward, when they were both blown into the air. His man was unhurt, but my man, Webb, has a hole hacked in his thigh which I syringe and pack every morning. The same man has been wounded once, and twice torpedoed, the second time was taken up by a rescuing ship unconscious from the sea and for a time he was doing orderly at Etaples – when he got this bomb wound. He's done his bit!

A boy in 'A' Ward tells me half the train he was in, was bombed – 150 or so casualties there alone – close to Etaples.

Another boy in 'A' (Hill), says he was in a ward of 15 beds, the men lying in bed on each side of him were killed or wounded – out of the 15. The same bomb was the cause of a boy's arm being torn open at the shoulder, a huge gaping wound, he is also in 'A' but was in a different ward to Hill – at Etaples.

The raid took place on Whit Sunday. On the following Friday, Etaples was bombed again – these men I've mentioned knew nothing of this as they left on Whit Monday. The first news we had of the second raid there, was when Sister Kirkham arrived here – she'd just about done her six months.

The St John's Brigade Hospital (which was untouched during the Whit Sunday raid) was terribly wrecked – 13 wards destroyed! 'Kirkie' saw the end of the ward next to hers crash down – and 10 were killed there. A man with a fractured arm was hurled out of bed almost into another ward – the shock and injuries were so great he died, poor chap. She ('Kirkie') said the floors of the wards at Etaples were made to pull up and dugouts had been formed underneath, these gave shelter to some, others had to lie under beds for protection – some crashed down and killed people – and one bomb fell onto a floor and through into one of the dugouts, killing a lot – poor things! Etaples is or rather was the biggest hospital centre (35,000 beds there).

Now to return to 'D' Ward and my month as 'Senior' there – I've enjoyed it very much. My men I've had are the following:

Trimmer – RGA	England – RAMC
Porter – Lancs Fusiliers Sgt	Webb – RAMC
Kennedy	Bentley – Cheshires
Campbell – A & S Hdrs	Davie – Scottish Rifles
Cpl Dickens – 4th Hussars	Childs
Kirkham – RGA	Caddick – KOR Lancs
McGee	Tyrrell – Leicesters

Tucker – RFA	Bugler – RE
Brown – A & C	Cleaver – 5th Lancers

I had 12 of these in the ward – the others (Convalescents) were in the 'tents'. 'Dickens' – ('Dickie' I christened him, and it was taken up by the rest of the men – and 'Dickie' it's been ever since) was a fine fellow (4th Hussars) – very badly fractured arm – he'd a great sense of humour and kept us alive. Trimmer had a wee stump of an arm left – which I took charge of practically all the time. Kennedy was perhaps the very worst case – awful back wound – deeply packed – with a tube in – fractured ilium and bad bed sore on hip – also a wound on the arm – it was a job moving him, and he lay all day and night on his tummy, poor little lad – and always moaned so when we did his dressings and syringed out his wound. One night when I was doing it – he sang – it made it worse in a way as one knew it was just to hide the pain, these plucky little beggars!

Caddick, a lad of 18 – shot through the shoulder – was a nice little thing – he's a long deep sinus (3 ins deep), you could feel the bone quite well when probing the wound and it had to have packing shoved right down into it for drainage, which hurt him a lot each day. I heard him describing an offensive – 'Bandoliers were dished out,' he said, 'I thought it was some offensive coming off, we were lying in an open field with nothing to cover, we. Eh, I was glad when I got 'it! I'd got me tongue out that far I'd 'ave got into a canal to cool me self, if it 'ad been further back.' We'd a particularly nice Colonel inspecting little Caddick – he smiled at him, 'Seen a bit of hell, have you boy – so have I, I was in a retirement, so I know!' Caddick was such a baby, somehow and looked too young to have been through what he had. One of the other boys shouted at him the other day – 'You're growing a 'tash (moustache), you can see the milk on it!' he'd just finished off a mug full.

Three of the worst ones we used to carry out – beds and all when it was warm and sunny – Kennedy, Bugler (a gastric ulcer man) and Tucker (gunshot wound in thigh) – the other boys used to pick them up and carry them just where I wanted them put – 'You're in command, Corporal, give your orders,' they'd laughingly say – 'You know we'd do anything for you!' We sometimes used to line up the beds underneath the end window – out on the grass, facing the trees (and the road!) where the girls used to pass. These boys and their 'birds!' as they call them – 'Dickie' used to be so fond of the 'birds', that I used to call him 'Dickie Bird!'

I heard a funny little conversation going on – 'Dickie' was looking down on the boys outside from the ward window – 'I say, why don't you roll up decent, so we can give you a decent burial! Any flowers? Why 'aven't you passed away yet, oh, you do die lovely!'

Sgt Bentley had a very bad knee – with three sinuses – and he dreaded some people (the Sister for one) to pack it – I did it nearly always myself – and knew the direction of the sinuses by heart – 'You're so gentle handed – nurse – you do my knee, I'd rather you – it's hurting but I'll not mind, I know you can do it alright,' and two or three times a day I used to do it for him – pull out the long ribbon gauze and stuff it in again afresh.

'There, look at that, a treat!' he used to say to the boys who finished packing his wound without making it bleed – 'and when that Sister comes she rams in the packing so tightly it streams with blood – and pushed so clumsily with the probe.' 'That Sister' (as he calls her) is only doing holiday duty, she's not one of our own sisters, luckily.

These 'D' Ward boys were always buying lettuces etc. for tea –

'Eh!' one said – 'If you're a good boy you shall 'ave an onion for yer tea!'

'Thanks, we're 'aving onions out tonight.' Came the reply (tea out that meant).

A tiny boy (5 ft if that) was always sneaking in from 'A' ward – 'That chap's taken a fancy to us,' I said once.

'Look 'ere – out o' this ward' they yelled at him (all in fun), 'Go and put yerself in the ash bin – or we'll use yer as a probe! Go on! Bringing all "A"'s dust into "D"! Clear out!' All this fell off 'Tich's' back, like water off a duck's.

'Nurse, 'ave a bit o' cucumber?' and to please them I've often had a bit – they're funny fellows and love you to join in their fun.

* * * * *

114

I've been very lucky in the operation line since I went to 'D' – as I come in for the 'A' Ward ops, Nurse Ward does not like them – feels the heat and ether too much and her junior nurses are too junior to have in the theatre – I've seen two shrapnel removings (out of 'A') and a re-amputation of a thigh – and an awful lump of lead taken out of an eyebrow close up to the eye (out of 'H' Ward). I held an arm while shrapnel was removed (the 'A' Ward op) – all the time, while the Dr dug away. I love the theatre work – and dear old Woodfin is very good at getting me in for them – Sister 'Jock' sent me a message from 'H' to go and be present at two of her ops – quite an honour – as I'd left 'H' for 'D' Ward. Nurse Dorothy returns to 'D' (she's been on 'nights' for a month) so I shall get a move I expect.

The list is up – the new 'staff' one – and I am in 'A' Ward (my old 'A'!) with Nurse Ward – and Sister Townend – quite glad to be still at that end of the hospital, I really like it best – 'H' is so dull and one never sees anyone – except the men and the ward nurses, and 'F' I hate. The boys in 'D' – don't like me leaving – I've found this in every ward I've been in.

'This is a serious matter, we shall have to get you transferred,' they'll say as they pass me working away amongst the new men. 'You brought back all those lovely flowers,' they say looking at the supply of Croston's best, at A's table – 'Yes, it's all very well, they wouldn't 'ave got all those if we'd kept our nurse!'

Even now a little 'D' Ward boy, Tyrell, will help me willingly to scrub 'A' Ward's bowls – and only this morning I said to him as I emptied the kettle – 'Laddie, fill it up again, will you?' (I was hurrying with dressings). 'Of course, nurse – anything for a lady – and you know, I'd do anything for you!'

A week went smoothly enough in 'A' and then news came that the painters were to start in the ward on Monday, first thing in the morning – we moved into 'B' on Saturday and 'B' into half of 'E'. Our work was still to come – Sunday morning came worse work! Convoy of 110 arriving Mon. Well 'B' could not start getting ready as we were in possession – and painters were at work in 'A'! At last orders came that we were to move, and carry all the empty beds out of 'A' through 'B' and 'E' into the recreation – oh, what a move, our backs were nearly broken. Woodfin saw us struggling and remarked – 'Those girls will be dead tired before the convoy comes!' and tired we were – still we got everything down and prepared beds for the new patients – keeping the ones vacant near the door – the beds were packed like herrings! Top, bottom and sides and a double row back to back down the centre – at 9 p.m. all was ready – pyjama suits – towels and soap – charts made out and a hundred little things which had to be thought of. To our relief – 13 new men were sent to us before any other ward got any and all were walking cases – a let-off for us (except old Woodfin had a hand in this as she had an arrangement of the entire convoy – Matron being ill in bed). We got those 13 to bed in no time (four wounds – the rest gassed – debility and PUO men).

The next morning was the great job – about 15 or 18 of our old men had to be dressed – some with bad wounds – no hot or cold water – every drop carried – luckily there was a gas jet where we could boil a kettle or we should have been done! Another draw-back – if you had any dirty water (and we had lots needless to say!) there was nowhere to upset it – except outside on the grass and then there was a hurricane of wind blowing so that you and your basin if you didn't take care – got shut in the door as you tried to get out. Such was life down there in the Recreation Room.

Next morning came the move back to 'A' – a business too but the boys gave a lot of help and we got back in course of time. Anyhow by the time the Major entered with Woodfin, all was tidy and at the word 'Party, Shun!' from one of our NCOs – the men stood very smartly to attention and with a pleasant smile the Major passed along our lines – with 'All comfy boys?' and I got a very nice salute from him myself as I stood at the top of the ward – and all was over.

Our new boys are up and about – except some who have high temperatures from 'flu, if we escaped we should be lucky. I am off duty for the day as I write this with 'flu. I was bending over one very 'fluey' man (with 103.2 temp) sponging him down the night before and I thought, now if anyone had a good chance of catching it I have, of course the next day I had a cold water shooting down

116

my back and temp of 100 – still I 'carried on', tucking up one man after another in blankets and hot water bottles – it will go through the ward now I expect, five or six men to have had it (or rather are having it) and another I heard this morning has 102 temp – so he's starting I suppose.

One of our newcomers is a funny little Irish man – Murray. ('Paddy' of course he's been in the ward from the first hour he entered.) He showed me with pride a French 'Croix de Guerre' he found on the battlefield – a beauty – with its gold star and green and red ribbon – Paddy amused me when he described his last conversation with his officer – 'The morning I was leaving, my officer he says to me – "Paddy Murray," says he – "I'm going over the top to win the Victoria Cross" – "that's alright, Sir," says I – "an' I'm going to get to Victoria Station"!' which suited him far better than a VC .

Paddy's S's are all sh's – 'Yesh Shister!' He dreams and chatters and moans and makes awful noises in his sleep – 'Done 'im, done 'im, done 'im,' he keeps saying, and then a sort of suppressed scream – a horrid weird cry. That feller must 'ave killed a Fritz the others say, as they come round his bed – and it's preying on his mind – better wake 'im. I sometimes ask them to leave him, as he jumps nearly out of bed he's so scared when anyone wakes him. He'll do this directly he falls asleep. We have to wake him in the end – 'Now Paddy, what were you dreaming about?' I say cheerily to him when he's sobered down and got over the fright.

'Oh, Shister shure I dunno at all – I daren't tell you – when I sleep I always talk an' creates a disturbance – shure I dunno where I was at all! Maybe I'll be wi' the angels soon!' and the next minute he's apparently forgotten his dreams (if he ever remembers them) and he is chatting to the other boys.

'Nurse, you know, it's worse if you've bayonetted a German and he may have done that,' a boy said the other day to me – 'It makes you feel sort o' sick, and you think a lot after it.'

I said a page or so back that I'm off duty with 'flu. Woodfin (as always) is a dear, and one can't be too grateful too – she never can do enough for me and no one could tell what she's like when one is ill – perhaps it's just because it's me, she may possibly do more for me. I'm not blind to the fact that she's devoted to her 'Traffie'. She'll creep down to my cube – one time with some port in a medicine bottle – another time she'll send a lovely tray of dainties – all ordered by her. Just now she came in with a shiny crinkling paper full of dates – 'I've been digging for these!' She laughed (evidently from Matron's stores, where likewise the port once resided!).

Sister Jock's been here – 'Better?' she laughed in her merry Scotch – 'I'm sorry, I thought we should have had a military funeral!' Just before she left she said – 'Good for the chest,' and at the same time threw a box of good 'Matinée' cigarettes on to my bed. Bless her kind heart. I've plenty of friends here – but none to equal my dear Woodfin, she's a friend and pal to be proud of!

By the way – she and Sister Jock have both won the Royal Red Cross for their services, bravo – both of them! That's the 4th RRC to come to this hospital and I hear other hospitals round about are very jealous of us – let them be!

This means Buckingham Palace for Woodfin and Jock. Matron and Mrs Smith have had theirs presented to them, it's a pretty decoration – cross with red and blue ribbon. 'Oh, Traff!' said old Woodfin a few days ago – 'Why haven't you been with us three years? Instead of two? I believe the girls with three stripes will get "MBE" (Member of British Empire), I'd love you to get something, you deserve it – you're sure to get something after the war!' I've got Woodfin as a pal – and I tell her I've the Red Cross to thank for that! And I can't be too grateful.

I've been in the theatre this morning – a bad knee operation – Dr Healey inserted four of the largest sized tubes (not only inserted, but through and out again), it's an ugly sight now, more like a porcupine than a knee, each tube stitched through the skin to keep them in place – it was a 'D' Ward op, Nurse Dorothy has 'flu – so I got in to it, in fact I was doing dressings in 'D' Ward when I was called into the theatre – I get 'A's and 'D's, (splendid!) as Nurse Ward won't go into the theatre and the 'D' junior 'daren't' or 'doesn't like.'

118

Woodfin laughed when she looked up as I entered the theatre – she and Taylor said, 'She's a brick isn't she, she's the only one, she doesn't mind a bit.'

There's a bad amputation in a few days time – in 'D' – wonder if I shall get that.

Since I wrote this I have been put 'Senior of "A"' – a 'push up'! Instead of amputation they are trying to save that leg (in 'D' Ward) – I was in at the operation – it took one and a quarter hours – putting in tubes and moulding the iron frame and plaster of Paris – My the mess (as besides all the gory mess of operation)! There were all the bowls of mixtures of plaster – floor, tables, sink, everyone's hands – everything covered up with it. Dr Collinson operated. The leg looks awful today – wound all bulging and hanging over onto the splint – and so swollen – I've been in 'D' assisting to lift the leg – he's in terrible pain of course – panting and sighing – with a temp of 102 – he at last said, 'Wouldn't it be champion to be well!'

I was the only nurse for 'A' and 'D' this evening – my feet feel tired – I must get them into some 'sea salt' – old Woodfin has some, I caught her soaking hers last night – we both get tired, hot, aching feet at times and make for the 'sea salt' – I really think it eases them – she's got a box of the stuff. 'Traffie, use it when you want, what's mine is yours, you know that,' said she. Good old girl!

* * * * *

'A' is not a bad lot just now – a willing crowd, and easy to get on with. Sister Kirkham is now my Sister – ripping having her! Like old times – Sister Ward has left – 'Kirkie' is a very good exchange for her! 'Paddy' still continues to amuse us – always singing (strings of verses of 'Parlez-vous' – seems to be his favourite!).

> 'The NCOs have a jolly good time
> Swinging the lead behind the line
> Hinky pinky, parlez-vous' or another verse.
>
> 'Madamoiselle from Armentiéres
> Hasn't been kissed for 30 years

The other boys take it up in a second – and fall in step and march away out of the ward singing it. We've a Taffy – Welsh Regt, who gallops off Welsh songs – 'Eh! Bet 'e's a Fritz,' they say laughing – then they jibe at him. 'The Bosch is fond of music – came down on 'em, they did, at Vimey and pinch the band – that's right they did!' (they say turning to me) 'They pinched the whole of the Welsh Regt's band – instruments and all! And off with 'em!' Again we strike up 'Parlez-vous' – some gay youngster will walk off with –

> 'The RFA have a jolly good time.
> Parlez-vous?
> Dropping their shells in our front line
> Hinky, pinky, parlez-vous.'

Funny fellows – and I think, funnier still songs.

Never shall I bring roses again into the wards, I'd a lovely lot – Croston ones in a bowl and they really looked fine for 10 minutes – it was 'Nurse, just one – this little bud, I wouldn't haven't taken one without asking you.' 'Oh, nurse (from two 'D' Ward boys) you won't mind two of your old boys having a bud each! Please nurse?' – 'Nurse is better than all the roses put together!' said another (I expect in hope of getting a bud!).

I was amused tonight, two 'B' Ward boys said to me at the ward door – 'Nurse, could you give Jock and me a photo of you – we won't tell 'A' Ward – we'd love one each!' Now I never said two words to these fellows – except perhaps a 'good morning' or 'good night' as I passed through – no more meant for them than any other of the 'B' boys.

One Sunday last I had three interesting hours in the operating theatre – one, shrapnel removing – and the other opening up an arm and inserting tubes – also five pieces of loose bone were taken out of it – the latter was Curnow – 'A' Ward. He was awfully sick and bad after and couldn't eat or fancy anything for two days.

We have a house now for convalescents, 'Grove House' – which is fed and staffed from here – it's about ten minutes' walk across the park – one Sister and three VAD run it – they can take in about 30 – in this way we can send on men to them – which eases us – in one way, though it's worse for us, as these convalescents are most useful in the wards fetching up meals, cleaning the ward, sweeping, emptying ash-trays.

The 'A' Ward boys – really sing awfully well in chorus – all taking parts, I often find myself humming and singing with them – it would do anyone good to listen to them, and some good voices too amongst them.

'God send you back to me
Over the mighty sea –
Dearest I want you near
God dwells above you –
Knows how I love you
He will send you back to me'

their voices rise and fall – the tenors and seconds and others all blending beautifully.

Just now as I write 'F' Ward is singing 'Genevieve' – just in the same way – the whole ward – it is 9.30 and I'm scribbling a page or two – as I'm alone – in my cube. Other favourite songs are 'Blue Eyes', 'Tennessee', 'Dixieland', 'Thora', 'Friend of Mine' and dozens of others – the ward has a mania for 'Parlez-vous' and will keep breaking out with a new version.

'Mademoiselle, have you got any wine
Parlez-vous?
Mademoiselle, have you got any wine
Parlez-vous?
Mademoiselle, have you got any wine
Fit for the boys in the fighting line
Hinky, pinky, parlez-vous!'

Funny chaps they always have some craze like this. The little Irishman left us two days ago, he was the starter of this aristocratic song! 'I'm going to leave you Shister,' he said to me, the night before – 'and when I go, think I'll cry and say Nurse Trafford's a very nice lady!' I trooped a dozen or more of Dr Bell's men up to the office and got them weighed today – a new 'weekly weighing' – a crack of this worthy Doctor's! Which I hope won't last long.

I bring up the evening letters sometimes – and call out names as I shuffle them about, sorting them. 'Any for me nurse?' from a bra' Scottie leaning over my shoulder – 'No, Jock, it's no use she loves another!' I say, finding there isn't one for him. 'Nurse, she's not true! What do you think?' 'Nurse, I think me mother's joined the "Wacks", got called up with the last group or something, I've not got a letter from her,' and so on. 'Oh Nurse, you're a "bon" post-man tonight,' from some lucky chap who seizes his letter in triumph!

I had two operations in 'A' today – I went in to one (bone scraping knee) four pieces of shrapnel in but it's gone well into the joint and unable to be removed. The other (dead bone), I let Parker go to – her first op. – she's my junior now. Hill began muttering 'Left! Left! Left! Right! Left! They're coming!' Germans on the brain again – poor boys they soon begin thinking and dreaming of them.

These two boys' beds were opposite each other – Harsley opened his eyes first and looked at me. 'It's all over, boy.'

'Not it, I've not been in yet – have I? Nurse, is it over?' he went on still holding on to my hand in a dreamy way – as I stooped over him – then – 'Nurse – oh, I'm sick,' and the usual!

Then Hill began to look round – 'Nurse, did I talk – did I say anything?'

'Not a word, Hill! How do you feel?'

'Oh I'm alright,' came the cheerful answer – and then shut his eyes. They were very quiet these two, not shouting and moaning like some – but then they'd only had a small amount of chloroform and ether, compared to some.

Tommy's smattering of French would amuse most people! 'Comment allez-vous?' is turned into 'Comment tallow candles?' and when they had influenza in most of the ward they thought it

122

quite a smart thing to say – 'Comment allez-flu?' Not so bad either!

When there's heavy fighting, 'Allenmand beaucoup bombard!' quite to the point!

'Nurse' – said Harsley the other day – 'Can February march?' ('Some catch coming' I laughed) – 'April, May,' he said and shouts of joy!

* * * * *

I've had some 'souvenirs' given me lately, great prizes to the boys – and I like to have them so long as they've got others left for themselves – I don't hold with them giving them all away – amongst others I had a necklace found in Bethune church, an Italian bullet – given to me by an RAMC who was right down with American and Italian armies near the Swiss borders – I also had some coins found under a stone in front of an altar in a church, two Canadians were found crucified, poor things! I've had two buttons promised to me, cut off a German – 'And nurse, the blood stains are still on them!' added Curnow – I got a little gilt anchor, evidently off a naval uniform from 'Paddy' who left a few days ago. I've had some money notes too – and a wee YMCA ticket – no value in itself – but it's been through no end of engagements, retirements, bombardments etc. – having been in the giver's pocket the whole time of his long service out in France.

We've had another convoy of 120 (July 17th) that is two nights ago – got to bed at 4 a.m. and up at 8 a.m. Tired aching feet therefore! These are a very good lot as far as dressings go – the heaviest convoy we've had for ages – large wounds and plenty of them. 'A' Ward had the honour of having the worst, this time – it's the first convoy I've had on my own – the first big one, I certainly had seven in 'F' and 'G' one night and six or eight while in 'D' – all the others I've been second in the ward or running jointly with another. This time 21 new men were sent to me – a grand lot – and I feel quite pleased to have been Senior when they came in. One boy (Bouillancy by name) has his back peppered all over (like a plum pudding) with shrapnel.

'Goodness, is that shrapnel?' one of us said.

'Yes, why are you surprised – what did you expect to see?' he said, turning his big bare back round for inspection. 'Has a frog feathers?' as if you could be expected to see such an uncommon sight. The expression amused me! A feathered frog!

Here are some more funny names – Ridout, Deerose, Love, Large, Joy, Brownjohn, Swift, Whiffin, Snowball, McKeating, Ribbons, Lipsome, Stenchcombe. Harsley made me laugh – tonight – he offered me a white tea rose he had in his buttonhole.

'Here nurse, you can have it.'

'I suppose a "bird" gave you that?' I said looking knowingly at him.

'No, not this time,' he said – 'Not a bird, it was an old rook – an old man! He was coming out of the park with some lettuces under his arm and I tried to cadge some for me tea – but nothing doing! Then I said, "That's a nice rose you have". "Yes, I growed it meself", he said, "You can have that!" (Old rook, instead of 'bird' – that time!)

'Nurse, I expect my sister and some friends tomorrow – I expect they'll come and bring us some "blinkin" strawberry.' They did as it happened – flowers and strawberries and the worst cases of nice tea.

'I once had a Trilby hat,' Horsley told me, 'and I looked like a robin under an ivy bush!' Suppose it was too big for him, these boys have such funny expressions.

July

I go on Monday for a fortnight's holiday – wonder where I shall be when I return – what ward?

August

I returned today to find I am in 'H' ward again. Heyhurst and I have it with Sister Johnson – not very busy now. Sister 'Jock' and 'Kirkie' are on night duty. Quite a nice lot of boys in – and a few left of my very old lot – who gave me a warm welcome.

Heyhurst, who's been with me for a fortnight has now gone and I have a junior – and am running 'H' – still under Sister Johnson – she's a nice little thing – very merry with a very Scottish accent – and easy to work with. I've known for a long time Woodfin wanted me to go with her to the sea – I didn't like to ask for a 'week off' to go with her, as I wanted to get a fortnight at home in September. Anyhow that good old girl went and asked Matron on her own – she is a brick! Well, one evening up came Woodfin, just bursting to tell me it was all settled – so we're going to enjoy ourselves. Woodfin told Johnson she was taking me away from her – 'How nice,' she said, 'but I'm sorry to lose her – you'll let me have her back in the Ward I hope!'

Well since starting this page, a lot has taken place – I've been away three weeks. One week, or rather ten days, at Robin Hood's Bay with Woodfin and the rest of the time at home – these weeks not being hospital life I shall not go into details and descriptions.

Here I am back in 'H' Ward. Easterby and myself – two convoys have come here since I've been away – and only about six of the old 'H' boys remain, the rest are in tents or gone to Grove House. Still another entry in this book – I'm told I'm to go on night duty – oh well there are many things about it I don't object to – and am always quite happy – it's a blessing to be without the rush of nurses and their worries and squabbles – they love me to death. I am to have 'H', 'E' and 'F' and 'G' Wards during the night (relieved by nurse Rigby) and from 5 a.m. I have charge of 'E'.

Here I am stuck on nights – 'E' Ward is the principal one to watch – Rourke who'd been operated on ... and was three hours in the theatre, because of haemorrhage – this afternoon – which meant me sitting many a weary hour by his bedside watching for the least stain on his bandages – and giving him wee sips of soda water through the night. The tourniquet was on ready to be screwed up – if it was necessary, it's a responsible job and one when I'm always thankful when morning comes!

They seem a nice lot of boys in 'E'. One week gone – and now the new attraction is an 'H' boy, Briggs – with a big scalp wound – he

125

went quite off it at times, and that rough, I had to get an orderly to sit with me as well – when I was relieved by another nurse he sent messages to me – saying 'Why had I gone away? Why had I left him?' All through one night he kept saying, 'Oh nurse, my head, my head! Take the weight off it do! do! (all the time putting up his hands over his head as if he wanted to lift something off) I can't stand it – it's more than I can stand! Oh, that weight! Oh it's cruel! Nurse finish me off – please do, put me out of my misery – do! Do! Please finish me off!'

I had a night or two of him and then he was transferred to Whalley! I always seem to have some beauty to manage while on nights! A Sister came for me in a hurry one night, when I went on duty – to ask me to go to 'B' Ward – two men were just out of theatre and the other night staff hadn't all arrived or finished their supper (or rather breakfast). So off I went – the one on the left hand had come round – but the one opposite was still 'well under.' I sat by him for a time and then a slight movement – 'Now, we're in for it,' I said to a man next door – 'We'll hear some tales.'

First he started sobbing, just like a little boy of six years old! Then quietened down and turned over – from that time he never stopped talking – he fired off with 'Allez! Allez! (Someone near thought he said Annie, Annie). 'Je vous aime, I shall pull through alright, I said I should! When we parted. It was not goodbye – only "so long". Oh mon pied – mon pied! Mal très mal! They must have eat the ankle bone away! Oh mon pied! Mon operation. It's alright, dad, old lad! There's nothing to worry – the very best of care and attention I have here – the nurses are nice – very nice. If I'd had a good education, there's no telling what I should have been – I'm a gentleman – a gentleman, spelt with a capital G! Those French sentences – the English language is the hardest to learn.' (This boy O'Neil is very keen on French and generally says something to me while passing through 'B' Ward, as he finds that I can talk French.) He went aimlessly on – rambling and muttering French sentences – till I left him and returned to my own part of the hospital with the 'B' Sister's thanks – and I told her I'd had an entertaining time!

The usual morning routine goes on in 'E' Ward – I get on well with the boys there – one of the day nurses informed me the other morning at breakfast – that her boys were 'very well satisfied with their night nurse!' This breakfast after night duty is a scramble some days – 'day nurses' and 'night', all wanting toast at once or marmalade and the later you are the worse for you – only the basin to scrape or not that, always! The other morning I sat holding an egg in my hand eating it with the end of a spoon, which was too big a size to fit, using it in the right way! Also no cup to be had therefore a soldier's pint mug held my tea and I was perfectly happy – a real picnic!

'Well Nurse de Trafford, you're no snob!' came from one of the day staff, 'and I wish there were more like you!'

I start getting the boys up soon after 5.30, the twists and shapes they get themselves into during the night are wonderful – you try and pull at the sheets and find head, legs and body are all rolled up in a long straight twist – 'Eh,' shouts a man opposite – 'Jock' Gordon by name – 'One more twist and he'd be a puzzle.'

'Must be related to a dormouse,' remarks another looking at him. At length the roll of sheet wakes – 'I'm all of a twist,' he mumbles.

'Yes,' I say laughing – 'Oliver Twist you mean!'

Gordon is a splendid help in waking up 'sleepers' – he's always up first and carries a boot which he holds over the bed threateningly – 'Eh, you – are you showing any signs of emotion? (always emotion!) – 'any flickering of eyelids?'

'Any more washings, nurse,' says an orderly – 'Yes,' says a man, 'A chap over there has no legs on, he'll want some!' (No legs on – such an expression!) Might as well say – something about a shirt that has no buttons on!

I saw a good operation the other morning (a mastoid) done by Dr Sykes – beastly looking sight – the op. was at 9.30 – and as I'd done a good bit in the theatre for Woodfin between 6.30 and then – I got let in for it – and I was glad – as it was the first mastoid I'd seen done. The Sister changed – Sister Cooper is on in Sister Johnson's place and Sister Wiggin is staying on for another month. I have Sister C, my end of the hospital – I am now promoted to Senior Staff Nurse! Write my own report – of 'E' Ward.

The time has gone on – and my month is up – and I'm back on days. The last evening of night duty a convoy of 60 arrived – Sister Hopkins (Hoppy) is the day Sister of 'E', and stayed up to receive the new men – I was her senior nurse therefore. Eleven new men came into 'E' – I made a list of temperatures, took names, and diagnosis of each case which I handed over to 'Hoppy' and helped her with several bad dressings – one man has eleven wounds (bombed by aeroplanes) poor chap. 'Hoppy' left the ward about 1 a.m. and I 'carried on' through the night – of course didn't get any time off and there were several likely cases for haemorrhage – which wanted special watching.

* * * * *

Well, I'm now Senior nurse of 'D' Ward, in Nurse Dorothy's place (she's gone on night duty). We are terribly, terribly, busy down there! Besides heavy cases in this new convoy – we have 'flu to contend with – really bad 'flu too! One of the juniors (from 'A') went off ill – so now Easterby (who's in A) and I (in D) have a junior to run between two – 40 men between us! The fact is that I am as much in 'A' as in 'D' after my dressings are done – I do all my own – I like 'D' for that, one always works so much on one's own and still have the 'A' Sister to fall back on for advice if you want it.

Sister Dunston has had 'flu and been off for a week – leaving us 'Sisterless' for three days till 'Johnson' was sent to us from 'F'. Woodfin came two mornings and did a few of the hardest dressings in 'A' and I got her to do two of mine – ripping having her.

On Sunday 'A' had three operations – and one done in the ward under ether, such a pandemonium and carrying on – having his leg opened – screens all round – Dr Sellers operating – Dr Murdoch giving the anaesthetic, Woodfin and Johnson, Easterby and I – beyond all this – there was Brown, very, very ill – temp 104.8 with 'flu' and pneumonia (he's been in the hut) and belongs to 'D', but I'm full up so they've given him an 'A' Ward bed – and I do his dressing – and look after him a lot – he's sponged down three or four times a day from head to foot and sheets and blankets and pneumonia jacket wet through as a sop each time with perspira-

128

tion – and he's frightfully weak – poor old boy, and as limp as a rag. He's such a job – all fresh blankets and clothes to be warmed and towels kept wrapped round hot water bottles to rub him down with, as we wash him. My, we are in the thick of it! And oh, how tired – but – carry on!

Poor Sister Wiggin has died – it's most sad – got influenza and pneumonia and was ill only a week. It's so strange to think she will never be amongst us again. I had been more with her than other nurses – but she's only been here for about six months, she was my sister, when I was in charge of 'A' – six months ago – came there on her first arrival and she's been on night duty while I was. Poor thing. Our big Red Cross flag has been at half mast – sad to feel she was lying dead here, in her little room off 'F' Ward. We nurses and sisters have sent a big wreath (she's been taken away to Staffordshire, to her home). The boys have collected nearly £10 – amongst themselves – nice of them! 'A' and 'D' Wards collected 35/-. 'H' Ward over £2. We've had about ten cases of 'flu – amongst the men and Sister Dunston has had it mildly – but is back with us in 'A' and 'D' now.

*   *   *   *   *

The 'D' boys I have are – viz:

Dickson – Argyle and S Highlanders – GSW Leg.
Auty – Devons – eight shrapnel wounds – legs and hand.
Jeffries – Bedfordshire Regt – Scalp wound.
Maloney – Manchesters – GSW leg.
Nugent - Durham Light Inf. – Shrapnel wound leg.
Pemberton – RFA – Shrapnel leg and chin.
Salisbury – York & Lancs – Blown off hand.
Lingard – Shrapnel wound thigh.
Morris – ROYLI – Wound arm.
McGregor A & S Hdrs. – Thigh and buttock wounds.
Wright – Amputated leg.
Murphy – Hand and finger.
Wells – Shrapnel, both legs.
Wells – Leicesters – Shrapnel in thigh.

They told me some awful stories of their experiences in France. Auty was 18 hours in a shell hole on a high road, and was saved from being killed by pieces of officers and men falling on him. His platoon officer – who'd just come out from England had ordered him to a dressing station as he'd been hit – when Auty looked at him again both legs were off – and head nearly severed – lying dead. The same boy, Auty, (Nauty as we call him) once saw an ammunition wagon, all horses dead, and driver dead, with reins still in his hand. Nugent saw one live horse standing pitifully looking round, the rest of the team all dead and all the men too – 'Jerries was coming, we couldn't stop to cut him free,' he said.

Maloney was 19 hours in a shell hole – shell came – blowing both horses and himself into the air. He was stunned and when he came round he found himself yards away in this shell hole and looking about, he could see the wagon (what was left of it) some distance away – horses blown to bits – that was a narrow escape if you like!

Shell-shocked horses they tell me are worse than shell-shocked men – no holding them, they just go mad and they'll stand a lot of shelling too. When they get badly shell-shocked they just cut them off – cut the traces through, and let them go.

Maloney said, 'I cut one loose one day and he galloped just anywhere – into Germany maybe! We never saw him again.'

Wright said (while talking on their experiences) – 'A man had 16 machine gun bullets in his chest, and lived three minutes afterwards.' They tell me very gruesome stories sometimes – it's rather awful, but here is one.

Maloney said, 'I saw a Bosche sitting in a shell hole, brains hanging over his face, he was working one hand and then the other up and down like a pump – he took his revolver out and fired just missing me and another chap, then he fell back dead.'

Another man, Auty, told me how he ran across some bare ground to take refuge in a shell hole – as he crouched there he saw a Bosche officer's arm hanging over with a beautiful ring on his finger – Auty felt for the ring and thought of drawing it off – but he said – 'The fist was half clenched and I felt as if the dead man was clawing the ring away from me – it gave me the creeps and I couldn't do it.'

They'll talk on for ages once they get a start – one against the other and I know what they say is true as they work themselves up so – and are so explicit about it.

I took two of my men to 'Stores' to get soft woolly shoes and never have I escorted such a lame pair there before – we all three laughed! They struggled along after me in some fashion, and opening the stores door I said, 'Pity these chaps and give them some soft shoes – look at them – did you ever see such a pair,' and looking back I saw one propped up against one side of the door-way, and one on the other!

'You look like an advertisement for Dones backache pills, fashion as yer walk,' remarked a man from a bed.

'I used to be able to run,' said Auty, 'in city life.'

'So did I,' said a boy standing on one leg with a foot of leg dangling in a long loose trouser leg – which although turned up and safety pinned above the knee, was far too long for what remained of his leg.

Poor beggars, and what spirits they have too – a boy in bed was drilling two boys on crutches the other morning. 'Parade, shun! By the right! Quick march!' Having got them across the ward, the order came, 'Halt! Mark time!' They used their crutches instead of feet – thump! thump! thump! thump! they went as they marked time, then right about turn – somehow they'd turn face to face for fun – and then a collision of crutches and roar upon roar of laughter from the occupants of the surrounding beds.

There has been such an amount of operations lately. I was in at one awful one (one of my men, Salisbury) the other day, the one with a blown off hand – Dr Collinson put in five tubes and cut it about tremendously – it's been so swelled up and was the size of three hands – just like a balloon – all sore and streams of matter running from it. It's going on well now – I dress it in the evenings – and syringe out the tubes with peroxide and eusol – and wrap it in gauze – also it has a splint to contend with, so it takes me a good time to finish him off.

'F' Ward gave a great concert a few nights ago – jolly good too. I hear another 'Pierrots' do is talked about – so some 'effort' will be required on our part!

*   *   *   *   *

Great excitement is astir! Will this armistice be signed? It is only a matter of a few days (if it comes off) – before we have peace! Too good to be true ------- November 10th – A day I shall never forget! -------- Matron arrived in the Ward saying --- 'Armistice signed at 5 a.m. --- all hostilities cease at 11 a.m.' --- a big cheer from 'D' boys and nurses standing near at the time --- then a minute or two to realise it --- then I think we went mad, or a near approach to it!

Off we went to the kit stores – tore open the old Christmas decorations boxes – cut off small Union Jacks which we pinned on our aprons and caps – Matron draped in a garland of red, white and blue paper – which I pinned up for her. Woodfin came and pinned a Union Jack on me – and we three and several nurses started a procession – headed by Quick (orderly) with his mop on high and he was followed by the band, that is a patient clapping two trays together making a most infernal noise – away we went all through the hospital. The procession getting larger and larger as we went – as other ward nurses tacked on to us – the old Matron was quite a sport. 'How do you think I'm to keep order, if I go through the wards in this get up!' she said. 'How am I to keep the men in order?' She laughed good naturedly though and quite entered into the fun of the day.

All this time mill hooters and bells – went screaming away, and we went outside and listened and could hardly make ourselves believe we had peace at last ---- 30 days allowed to decide is the condition – very stiff conditions too – to clear out of Belgium and France, give up all prisoners, 5,000 guns, 1,000 aeroplanes, and goodness knows what else. So at Christmas time (six weeks' time off) we ought to hear of real peace.

My time (1 month) in 'D' Ward is up and I'm back in my old 'A' again, there I hope I shall stay till we close the hospital. I spent a very happy year (the first year I was in the hospital) in 'A', and I always feel so at home there. At present Easterby is with me – and we take alternate days to do dressings. Sister Johnson is my Sister. We've had two convoys, not very big ones, about 60 men each time. I like the 'A' boys very much. Some of the nicest are:

Caruthers	AB Moore – HMS *Anson*
Wardle	Davidson – Gordons
Stewart – Camerons	Brown – RGA
Sgt Hingle	Keighley – MGC
Jones – RGA	Baker – RGA
Graham – A & S Highlanders	Swinhoe
Oates – Manchesters	Christie
Holland	Lawrie – Black Watch

The committee have behaved vilely lately, in such an underhand way. They arrange things without consulting Matron, they even waited till she was away on a few days' holiday, to hold a meeting to decide on closing the hospital – on the grounds that 'The VADs were tired,' and that 'Funds were wanted'. Matron being one of the committee, it was odd to arrange this without her being present. We VADs were up in arms, naturally, about being 'Tired' – as not a single girl wished to leave and we are all devoted to the place and our work.

As for funds – we have £2,500 in the bank at the present time and as the Government pays two-thirds of the upkeep of the hospital, that sum would last us several months more without appealing for further money from the Preston people. The hospital is well staffed and everything is running so smoothly and well, it seems a shame to shut down the place, especially now – as men from distant hospitals are allowed transfers quite easily (they used to be very hard to get).

Now if the place is closed, Preston boys will have nowhere to go except the 'Fulwood Military' or 'Whalley' where there are no comforts, such as a VAD one can give them – and all this money has been collected and given by Preston people – so that it seems hard if their own boys are not to benefit by it. We are Whalley's biggest VAD, and we are a primary hospital. Very few VADs have had trains of wounded from France as we've done.

The committee wrote straight to the War Office not even consulting Whalley, I believe Whalley is mad about this. Maj Robinson (officer in command) said they would have kept us full to the end of May. The old committee are just tired I suppose and want to shake themselves clear of the job – but they've not acted in the right way. Men from the hospital, outsiders, VADs and unknown writers, have written long letters in the *Lancashire Daily Post* – protesting strongly against the closing and the way the committee are going on.

We are to close February 1st – unless things can be altered, which I hope and pray may be!

*　*　*　*　*

We have had a busy time during Christmas – Easterby has left me in 'A' (her sisters being ill) and Hayhurst has now come to me – and we work it together. Sister Johnson left the decorations entirely to me – it was extra exciting this year – Matron offered a prize for the best decorated ward – I brought the draperies (bright Saxe blue gauze) which I festooned across the ward – the whole way down – making a blue roof or sky, from which we hung silver stars – it really looked well, then we had evergreens too – and silver frosting stuff. The whole effect was blue and silver and the red and white striped bed quilts contrasted very well. Six of my boys helped me and very willing they were.

'Nurse, you shall get first prize,' they said as they worked away – 'And if you do, we'll give you such a cheer.' My word we got it too! Eight Wards competed and extremely good they all were. Mrs Riddell (doctor's wife) judged them and returned to 'A' to tell us that we'd won it – as being the most original and best thought out. The boys clapped, and ran and shook me by the hand – with 'There, nurse what did I tell you? I knew you'd get it.' I got a man from the town to photograph it, also my boys (a big group of them) in the recreation room – with Sister Johnson and myself and Hayhurst – also I caught Woodfin and made her come in the centre of us all – this photo came out beautifully.

The Christmas this year outdid all others at Moor Park. Matron did

134

us finely – no end of luxuries and good foods – Christmas tree, bran pie, dances, concerts etc. We had a splendid fancy dress ball. Woodfin again getting an easy first prize for her Rajah's get up.

We nurses had a concert – which went with a good swing. We had the 'Hospital alphabet' again – with variations and changes to suit a fresh lot of Tommies. I was the leading one of four girls – and started off with "A" is for "A" Ward, that won the first prize with the decorations, and stars in the skies.' (Shouts from my 'A' boys). My verse – ' "M" is for Matron, our first RRC, we wish her good luck, and all prosperity' – also brought down the house. I took part in three other character songs and choruses – 'Smoke Clouds' – was about the best, (an oriental tableau).

I went home for the night and felt terribly cold – my room damp wet and bed cold and not aired enough I suppose – anyhow – although I slept in woolly coats and stockings! I felt miserably cold – I got a chill I suppose – awful throat – rheumatics all over me and temperature 102. Woodfin looked after me all the time – I was in bed in the cubes over a week, and then they moved me to the Sister's sitting room in the hostel – a very nice empty room and after being thoroughly 'spoilt', and fed on luxuries, I was once more myself and well again – and went home for 2 or 3 nights – returning to my old 'A' Ward.

*　　*　　*　　*　　*

The wards are closing now – one after the other – very sad – still it must be, and after all it's what we expect. 'F' and 'H' are shut, the men they had, left, have come into 'E', 'B', and 'A' – so we are full up again in these three wards. We've got a sailor – an AB named Moore – of HMS *Howe* – with a very bad leg wound, great piece of bone missing – a wretched slow wound that won't heal – his home is in Norwich (of course he's christened the canary!) His leg has no muscle in it – and it is like a stick – 'What a leg,' I remark, while dressing it – 'About as thick as my arm!'

A Scottie standing near shakes his head knowingly and says in a cheerful way, 'Never mind if it is a small leg – "little is guid" .'

This boy, Moore, has made a lovely belt – with regimental and naval badges mounted on it. He's so fond of saying, when I bring him a mug of tea, or some such thing, 'You're a toff, Nurse.'

A group stood round me, as I swathed a man's hand up in bandages – and much to the men's amusement (not mine at the time!) I found the fat hand refused to go through his sleeve! 'Eh! 'E's like man as built a motor in 'is back kitchen and he couldn't get it out after it!'

Dorothy Toulmin and I have been in 'A' for a week or two (her Ward, 'D', is shut). She and I were in the Nurse's Room with one or two others – a few days ago – when Matron walked in – 'I want Nurse de Trafford to go to 'E' Ward,' she said. 'There's a case of measles there – which I'm isolating and must send the 'E' nurse to look after it in 'G' Ward.' So after bidding farewell to 'A' (I hoped not for too long), I began work in 'E', under Sister Dunston – I was the only nurse – five boys, nearest to the measley boy (Capendale) – were put into 'F' Ward which was empty – I had the ward to look after in 'E', and the five isolated ones to feed – or rather take food as far as the door in 'F'. Plenty of fetching and carrying.

We continued like this – and I still remained in 'E'. No more cases of measles, except one of the masseuses – Miss Holland – who is now on leave in Liverpool, she's got it. She used to massage Nuttall, who was in the next bed to Capendale. They are a rough lot of lads in 'E' now – only a few really nice ones, and the five now in 'F' are decent fellows. I wish I was back in 'A', and the boys there want me. 'Sooner you come back the better!' the 'Norwich Canary' greets me when I pass along 'A' on my way to the stores. 'Here comes our nursie,' from another boy. 'We're lost without you,' and so on.

I spoke too soon –! Bryning has got measles – a voice said over the cube passage. When I returned from church on Sunday, 'Traffie I've got the measles.' 'Oh have you!' I replied quite cool and calm. 'Now I thought, I'm next or Anderton.'

We three, Anderton, Bryning and I have been down in these cubes together breathing the same air, as all walls are open 2 ft from the ceiling. After breakfast Bryning was isolated to a sister's room opposite 'G' Ward – where Capendale's nurse could look

136

after both cases. This gave one more work, as Nurse Fisher (who'd been operated on for a hernia) had been looked after by Bryning – Matron said, 'Nurse de Trafford had better take on Fisher.' My hands are full now – full enough before this addition. (I forgot to say I was in the theatre for Fisher's operation, quite interesting, the second operation for hernia I'd seen.)

Such a big lot of men left this morning, nearly 30! This has emptied us a lot. 'A' is empty now, moved into 'B'. So 'B' and my 'E' and the few isolated ones in 'F' are the only wards open. The end of the hospital is certainly coming quickly! It's horrid to think of. The latest order is ' "E" Ward is to close' – my five boys in 'F' are safe now – and are to go to Whalley in a day or so's time.

A cold, but beautifully sunny day – Woodfin came to me saying. 'Traffy, you and I will go on the ambulance – the 'F' boys are going to Whalley this afternoon.' So we got on the box seat and escorted the men there (a 15 mile run). This was my second run there on the Red Cross ambulance. They hated leaving – these boys, they'd been with us a long time. An orderly met them at the door and Woodfin handed over their papers – and after we'd said 'Goodbye' and shaken hands with each – they disappeared up the steps and through the big doors – looking back at us – as if to say 'Take us back!'

It is a funny place now and my what a job it is packing away 'E' Ward and carrying medicine bottles, and dressings and what not, back to the stores. All the locker and window curtains, Hayhurst and I washed and ironed! But she has gone now (finished for good).
   My feet are 'real tired' with so much running about here, there and everywhere! There is still Fisher (convalescent, but wants her meals brought) and Bryning with the measles and her nurse must be fed – and practically everything she requires – eatables, stores, washing, drugs etc. I have to carry up outside her room.
   I was to have left the hospital this week – but owing to the measles – Matron says I can't go home for a fortnight (at least a fortnight from the last case of measles – Bryning). Having

finished clearing 'E' Ward – between my waiting on the sick nurses! – I was put on to inventory work – spent about three days in medical stores – sorting bandages and making lists of cupboards – pages and pages of things! I offered to do any job, where help was wanted most, as I had no ward – and one day they were very short of 'washers up' in the scullery, I volunteered and after that I began to take root in the kitchen and for 10 days I worked away there – quite happily, sometimes Woodfin or Jock or one of the office girls would come in and laugh like anything – at me, arms covered with flour – making the pastry! or scouring down the huge kitchen table and dressers or sleeves rolled up doing my two hours' 'washing up' with hands like a washer woman's, all white and wrinkly.

'Let's see your hands, Traff! Will they ever come right?' remarked some spick and span little nurse, who looked as if she'd come out of a band box (being one of the office staff she could afford to look like this!) 'Oh, don't you trouble, they'll soon get right!' I said – 'Come and have lunch in the office,' they'd say sometimes – and a few times I'd go – but I was generally in a mess, big kitchen apron covering me up and greasy hands or soap in my nails! I used to find I was much happier eating my bit of (11 a.m.) lunch standing up round the kitchen table with the cooks and orderlies – munching a thick ham sandwich – a cup of coffee in the other hand. I learnt quite a lot in the cooking line and it was a change from the ward work and the kitchen staff were exceedingly nice to me. 'There's not a lady in this hospital as would have done what you've done,' remarked one of the cooks to me one day. 'Nonsense,' I laughed, 'I enjoy it all!'

I found one of the char women (one of the 'Mother's Mops,) at work, over 100 pots and pans, cups, mugs, plates, etc. etc. – 'Come on – I'll give you a hand – which will you do – wash or dry?' 'Eh, here comes Nurse Trafford, bless her,' replied the old lady, and together we soon made the mountain of pots less. From that job, I'd get put on working the mincing machine or chipping potatoes or doing the sheep's head soup. Any old job! To make a variety to my kitchen work and waiting on invalids – Matron discovered 'H' Ward curtains weren't taken down and 'F's wanted washing, they also had to be ironed, which took me ages! The screen chintzes had to be taken off, and there were ever so many little odd jobs I could do, being one of the last ward nurses in the hospital! All the others except Dorothy Toulmin had left (and she now has 'B' Ward, the only ward).

Matron said to me one morning, 'Well what have you been doing, washing up?'

'Oh yes, I'm a jack of all trades now!' She laughed good naturedly and said, 'A very useful person too! I don't know what we shall do without you!' She had me with her taking down the kitchen inventory – an awful undertaking.

One day Woodfin had me in the operating theatre – writing down lists of the instruments – also together, we polished them all – a lengthy job. That night when I was undressing the telephone rang, Would I go up to the office and help with the inventory of the ward instruments? Poor old 'Jack of all trades'!

The massage department is on such a big scale now (nearly 200 men coming each day for treatment) that they can manage to run a ward for pensioners – Preston men, whose wounds break down – Matron and Woodfin are staying and 'Jock' till June, (who takes the ward of course). Matron is asking the senior nurses to take one month's duty in the ward, in turn, and has given me May – it is now March so I shall have six weeks or more at home. I don't think by what I've seen that these pensioners will be as nice to nurse and 'do for' as the Tommies we've had straight from France – they have been home, and through hospital more than once before and they don't appreciate so keenly what we can do for them as these first boys did. They are apt to stay out – and 'not being a war on' as they say we have to treat them more leniently. All we can do is to give them three days' CB – which I don't fancy they mind much. I saw one fellow in bed the other day.

'Hullo Milner, in bed? Why's this?' I said.

'I've been a naughty boy,' he said cheerfully. Another chap sat twiddling his thumbs in bed (kept in on CB). 'I 'ope Matron's dog eats 'er canary!' he was muttering – out of spite I suppose for being kept in bed. Well so ends my three years' hospital life, and

139

I've loved it all – and am only too sorry it is ended, now back at home!

May

Sees me back at work in 'F' Ward (the ward we've been allowed to keep), 30 beds. There are seven massage sisters, and one VAD in the Massage Room – and one Sister (Sister Jock) in the ward and one VAD. They didn't know which to give me – ward or massage room, and in the end they thought the latter would be easier and lighter work for 'Fisher' who's the other VAD – as she hasn't long recovered from the operation she had done here. Jock and I have 16 men in the ward – and we are very busy in the mornings, especially – afternoons and evenings are slackest. A paralysed man – shot in the back (Ormrod) is the one who keeps us busy – he's really terrible at times and can't do anything scarcely for himself. 'Fowler' is another bad case – fearful legs – knees growing together – rubbing each other and his legs and feet sticking out like fins on each side, no room to pass him in 'G' Ward passage if by chance you meet him there – he's on crutches of course and for a certain time every day he has to lie with a knee tied to each side of his bed to try and bring them apart. He goes through it too, poor chap!

We've a lot of shell shock and heart cases – and men whose wounds have broken down again. Woodfin and I had a small operation on our own with Dr Derham (pensioner's Dr) the other day. 'Jock' was away (half day). Just gouging out a big lump from a man's forehead – a very bleedy messy job too – it was Sgt Carthey, an old patient, who used to be in 'B' Ward.

Such a lot of the old boys keep coming in to look us up – five the other morning. 'Jock' and I roared with laughing, every time we looked up from our work we seemed to see some familiar face at the glass door. 'Thought I'd walk round to look you up!' They walk their babies round too – more than we can do with at times! One's always glad to see one of the old Tommies – but they do look so different in mufti – it takes all one's time to put a name to them!

*   *   *   *   *

140

I've got appendicitis I'm sure – sort of 'stitch' pain and I feel blown out on the appendix side and can't hurry or run – dancing, tennis, etc. are quite out of the question – they advise me here (Matron, Woodfin and Jock) to get it seen to – and Matron is going to ask Dr Collinson to come up to examine me. I have only about one more week of my 'month in the ward' to run – I'm very glad to have been able to 'carry on' in spite of my appendix! Bedmaking is about the worst for me, and stooping, and I can't lift weights – it's a nuisance and a great drawback.

Well, Dr Collinson came up to see me, and he says by what I tell him, he fancies it must be appendicitis and says I ought to be operated on before I get a really bad attack and I quite agree! It's all arranged and settled, Matron is allowing me to be done here – I am glad! All amongst people I know – it will be so much nicer than going to the Infirmary or a nursing home. Dr Collinson will operate – Dr Murdoch will give the anaesthetic and Dr Derham has already promised to be present – and two Sisters, Woodfin and Jock – so if I'm not looked after well, I ought to be! Having no theatre – 'G' Ward is to be used (being empty), and it's quite nice when all cleaned down and sponged, and the empty beds covered up with clean white sheets – I've had it to prepare, so know how clean and nice it looks. It's funny to think I shall be operated on the very table (from the theatre), I've seen so many Tommies cut up on! And to be put on a Tommies' bed (my own mattress and sheets of course) and be nursed by Red Cross Sisters – in a Tommies' ward – a good enough ending to my three years in hospital.

Well – here I am – minus my appendix – I'm 'not all there', they say! Dr Collinson wasn't sure it was appendicitis, so made a bigger slit than necessary for the usual operation. Five inches long – and rootled about all amongst my inside – doing this has given me a lot of extra pain and bruised feeling – still it was as well to make sure.

As it happened it was my appendix, which was an inch longer than anyone else's – and had a fine fat grape pip reposing in it! I've now got my lost appendix bottled – and I'm very glad it's there and not in my inside!

They've all been very kind to me – Woodfin has done every stitch of the nursing herself – I was three-quarters of an hour under chloroform – and came round an hour after that. The three deep stitches were taken out in four days' time – and the rest (sewing the skin on each side of the wound together – in about twelve days' time – twelve of the latter. I stayed in 'G' Ward for three days – and then Matron went for a fortnight's holiday – and gave me her own bedroom during that time – which was very decent of the old lady. From here I went to my cube in the hostel, and used Woodfin's room (being a nice sized room) to sit in, in the daytime.

Altogether I was four and a half weeks convalescent there at the hospital and returned home to Croston – where I've just been for ten days – Woodfin returned with me for a few days – she's been indoors so much on my account – the change and outdoor life did her no end of good and later on she and I are going to a little Scottish seaside place – which will be a nice change for us both. I can walk very well and am out all day, my stitch holes and my inside are still sore and bruised, they say I shall feel this for some time, and it is only what one can expect. I'd even go back on duty to the good old hospital, I'll add a 'postscript' to this book – It's quite funny to be 'out of work' and at large again. Dr Collinson never charged me a penny for operating, being a VAD, and all the nursing I got free, of course. Woodfin did it all she said – just because she was so fond of me – 'her Traffy'.

November 1919
Received a coloured enamel medal – for my war services – St John's Badge by the side of the Red Cross hung from a scroll 'West Lancashire.' Very proud of it too I am (Regt No. 5973).

November 21st
They put me up at the hospital for a huge reunion of our Division of St John's – funny – but nice to be back in a wee cube again and everyone so nice and pleased to see me again. Four hundred nurses and ambulance men met in the Public Hall and were addressed by the Major and our own doctors and thanked for our services. We had a good ball – 8 p.m. to 1 a.m., and excellent supper. I hope to do a month's voluntary work for good old Moor Park

142

in January. They have taken back old 'A', 'D' and 'B' Wards, so the hospital is growing! Three wards, these will be, beside the massage work.

December 1919
Passed a higher exam for a Bronze Medal and my 'Medallion' a few days ago – Matron was anxious for me to try for it, thought I could manage it alright. Dr Holden examined me – quite enjoyed it.

January 1920
Just done a month's ward duty. Enjoyed it.

Went into 'F' Ward – Sister Arnott and worked with Donlan – for the first 10 days – 30 men, in ward. Then old 'A' Ward was opened – for surgical cases and Sister Arnott went to it taking me with her – and till the time I went we worked it together, I being the only nurse. 'B' Ward also sprung into life again – the doors opened and we two had both 'A' and 'B' to manage, 36 patients altogether, only four empty beds. Saw four operations while there – two amputations and two bone scrapings. The theatre is once more in use – it's like the old days being there. The tea for 100 out-patients went off well – also a staff ball in the big Massage Room. Everyone delighted to see me back again and I've loved my time there in 'A' and 'B'.

To finish my book I'm the proud owner of the Royal Red Cross, a King's decoration.

June 22nd to 24th
Two days as theatre nurse – two operations each day – two appendicitis cases and one hernia and one double hernia.

'To My Hospital'

1) Three happy years –
   Three years of the best –
   I know I shall feel their loss!
   Three busy years, of real hard work.
   'neath the wave of 'The Crimson Cross.'

2) A happy smile, and a cheery word –
   Met you whereever you went –
   You might feel tired – but they carried you on
   To the end of a day, well spent.

3) The 'Crimson Cross,' the
   Flag of 'St John's' –
   They waved there side by side
   As the men we nursed with pride.

                    E. de T.

The Wounded and the Fallen

   We've paid in our toil and our woundings;
   We've paid in the blood we've shed;
   We've paid in our bitter hardships;
   We've paid with our many dead.

                    John Oxenham.

   To live in hearts we leave behind
        Is not to die.
                    Campbell

Hospitals

The honour of being first in the field to offer local accommodation for the wounded soldiers belongs, I believe, to the Sisters of the Mount Street Hospital, who at a very early date set apart 14 or 15 beds for this purpose. That this patriotic act was appreciated by the public of Preston was shown by the liberality with which the hospital funds were supported.

The help afforded by the Royal Infirmary was on a more extensive scale, and for some time as many as 100 cases received attention there. The value of the treatment was enhanced by the completeness of the Infirmary equipment.

But the most valuable contribution of all was that made by the Voluntary Aid Detachment. For some time there was no scope for their activities owing to the lack of suitable accommodation for temporary hospital purposes. But their opportunity came when it was intimated that the principal pavilion used by the Royal Lancashire Agricultural Society for the purpose of their annual show was at the disposal of the VAD for the period of war. The pavilion was promptly transferred from Blackburn to a site at the north-east end of the Moor Park and with some adjustments and adaptations it was quickly converted into a hospital for 35 patients, with the necessary accessories. The site chosen was ideal. A belt of trees shut out all reminders of a busy manufacturing town, though a glimpse of the towers of the Grammar School might be caught across the park. But while the spot selected was sufficiently secluded to suggest a remote country place, the hospital was in fact near enough to the tramway to afford opportunities to patients to get quickly into the heart of the town – opportunities of which they readily availed themselves. The hospital as it began was, as I have said, a simple pavilion, but this pavilion threw out all sorts of shoots until it became quite an important institution, so complete in every respect that the Chief Lady Superintendent of the VAD after a tour of inspection pronounced it one of the finest in the land.

The seven stages in the evolution of the hospital seem well worth recounting.

First. – The Agricultural Pavilion having been provided as a nucleus, Messrs Horrockses (employers and employees) proceeded to extend it and to provide furniture and equipment (later this came to be known as 'D' Ward).

Second. – Mr Galloway added an isolation ward with a nurses' cloak room.

Third. – Mr Wm Parker provided an operating theatre.

Fourth. – The North Lancashire Cotton Spinners' and Manufacturers' Association built a new Ward ('E') with a dining room and new kitchens.

Fifth. – Mr Galloway put up a recreation room, and later a room for massage treatment and wound dressing.

Sixth. – Messrs Horrockses added two further wards ('F' and 'G') with equipment complete, and, making use of a small pavilion which had been lent by the Agricultural Society to the Loyal North Lancashires when in camp at Weeton, proceeded to extend it and convert it into Ward 'H'.

Seventh. – (The last stage of all, Mr Wm Birtwistle made a solid contribution in the form of a hostel affording accommodation for 17 nurses.

When this was completed the hospital provided beds and equipment for 174 patients. During the year 1918 further temporary accommodation was secured, and as many as 270 men were under treatment at one time, the total number passing through during the year being 1,150.

The establishment of the Moor Park Hospital relieved the authorities of the Infirmary from the necessity of diverting their accommodation from its ordinary purposes, but they continued to place their very elaborate equipment at the disposal of the VAD for special cases.

The work of this Hospital came to a close at the end of March 1919, though the buildings provided by Mr Galloway for massage treatment and wound dressing continued to be used for disabled soldiers sent there by the Pensions Committee. Several seriously disabled men were transferred to the hostel at Ashton.

In the year 1915 the Order of St John of Jerusalem organised a hospital for work in France, and Lieutenant-Colonel Trimble, who until January of the previous year had commanded our local Artillery Brigade, made an appeal throughout the area, which comprised the Counties of Lancashire, Cheshire, Westmorland and Cumberland, and the Isle of Man, for funds in support of its equipment and maintenance. Originally the hospital was offered to the War Office for six months, but such was the liberality of the response to Colonel Trimble's appeal – £18,105 being contributed within a comparatively short period – that not only was a magnificently appointed institution provided, but it was able to carry out its beneficent mission continuously from September 8th 1915. An authority described the hospital as the Show War Hospital of the World.

In the month of May 1918, it suffered very severely from enemy aircraft, the attack resulting in many casualties. For his 'conspicuous gallantry' in connection with these raids the Colonel (who had already been made a CB) received the Gold Life-Saving Medal of the Order of St John of Jerusalem.